Published by Tactical Space Lab, 2018 Sydney.

ISBN: 978-0-646-99587-8
Editors: Josh Harle, Angie Abdilla, Andrew Newman
Designer: Reese Geronimo

ACKNOWLEDGEMENTS

This project has been supported in partnership with Old Ways, New, an Aboriginal owned and managed cultural and technology consultancy. Old Ways, New is supporting the development of next-wave, Indigenous technologists; through the research and development of new, deep technologies based on Indigenous Traditional Knowledge Systems.

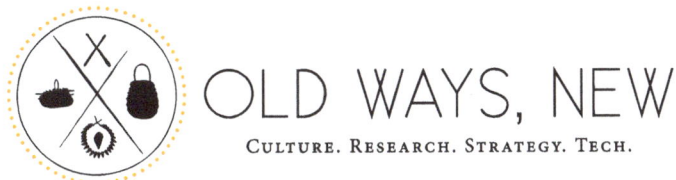

This project has been assisted by the Australian Government through the Australia Council, its arts funding and advisory body

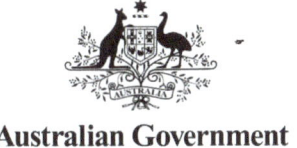

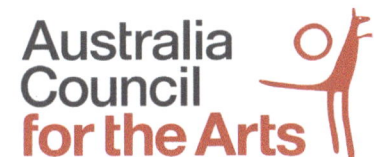

DECOLONISING THE DIGITAL
TECHNOLOGY AS CULTURAL
PRACTICE

EDITORS
JOSH HARLE
ANGIE ABDILLA
ANDREW NEWMAN

CONTRIBUTORS
ANGIE ABDILLA
THOMAS APPERLEY
MAHLI-ANN RAKKOMKAEW BUTT
FRENETIC STUDIOS
GENEVIEVE GRIEVES
JOSH HARLE
RHETT LOBAN
RAMSEY NASSER
AMANDA JANE REYNOLDS
CURTIS TAYLOR
TYSON MOWARIN
LYNETTE WALLWORTH

DESIGN
REESE GERONIMO

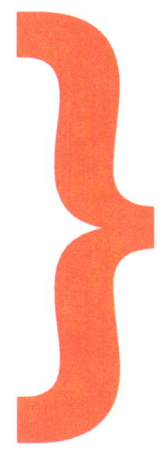

CONTENTS

INTRODUCTION

This is a book about storytelling: the stories that we tell to make sense of the world and share knowledge, and how these stories determine the ways we live. Storytelling composes knowledge and gives context to our existence, and embedded in these stories are the values and perspectives held by the communities that tell them.

In Australian Aboriginal culture, Songlines map the vast lands of the continent, its seasonality, plants, animals, the animate, inanimate and interrelated meaning and contexts. These Songlines — from creation stories to new stories — are activated through ceremony, rites, rituals and protocols, and embody deep knowledges which vibrate through Country, kin, and Aboriginal technologies.

Digital consumer technologies give us new ways to tell stories, ways that allow us to immerse the audience and share them with people across the planet, but these technologies are part of their own story, one that jealously defends its dominance and perpetuates a view of the world that privileges the few at the expense of all others.

The technologies we use impact our lives through implicit worldviews baked in to their operational logic. They aren't neutral instruments, but a human endeavour, and their intended purposes, capabilities, and acceptable uses are shaped by the cultural landscape from which they are manifested. Western science as a 'grand-narrative' is interlinked with colonial power, and has driven technological development according to its own values and understanding of the world, distributing the benefits and costs of technology unevenly according to a familiar map of European empire, and nourishing and propagating technologies that conform with its drive to 'capture'.

In practical terms, inclusion in the set of voices and stories told with this technology is not universal: they may be prohibitively expensive to access, and their usage is tightly regulated to preserve a model of consumption (where otherwise sophisticated technologies are actively designed to restrict free creation by users). The way a technology represents the world (its aesthetics) may embody hidden politics that insinuate themselves into the meaning of even expressive outcomes (e.g. the map assumes the legitimacy of its reductive, 'objective' account of the world), and they may, intentionally or unintentionally, exclude certain people from full participation through decisions made in their design.

In this book we argue that technology is not a neutral tool, but the application of a particular culturally-specific set of knowledge to solve a (perceived) problem. *Technology is a cultural practice.* Through the book's four contributed papers, we explore the legacy of Western colonialism and how it manifests through the landscape of contemporary technology.

In doing so, we are arguing for the importance of 'decolonising the digital'. In broad terms, 'Decolonising' describes a process of disentanglement from colonial power, seeking independence and self-governance: "creating and consciously using various strategies to liberate oneself from, or adapt to, or survive in oppressive conditions".[1] Decolonising is an ongoing process. It is the active awareness of the pathology, implicit discrimination, cultural assumptions, and bias within Western systems and the championing of the repressed and silenced voices/knowledges/histories which challenge the historical narrative that excluded them.

Through this book we propose a framing of 'technology as cultural practice', describing the historical backdrop and contemporary operation of Western culture in forming mass-market technologies. This culture, co-created through the Enlightenment and intimately tied to mechanisms of colonisation, sets up a paternalistic 'responsibility' to withhold agency through control and oppression, not just of colonial subjects, but anyone not fitting the historical archetype of the rational agent (e.g. women). The crisis of colonial culture still at play in modern science and technology affects everyone. It's evidenced by the proliferation of profoundly unsustainable, environmentally destructive industrial technologies, and emerging digital technologies that narrowly benefit the world-view of a privileged few to the exclusion of others.

The claim to universality of Western science is fundamental to its use as a tool of dominance, and hides its subjectivity, cultural-sitedness, and Eurocentric perspective. Because of this, the project to 'decolonise the digital' addresses not only brutal colonial history — the violent enforcement of behaviours and prohibition of practising Indigenous technologies, for example — but intellectual integrity and perspective, responding to the historical erasure of diverse voices from the dominant historical account. This myopic view of the world should be of concern to everyone, especially against a backdrop of the enforced dominance of Western science and technology which continues to reproduce bias and inequality at a cost to the environment.

For those whose existence, stories, and cultures have been historically excluded from consideration in the development of technologies (e.g. languages not available, faces not recognised), the manifestation of culture through technology and science is abundantly clear. For them, this book may be seen more as a rallying cry for the value of diverse perspectives. Contemporary art practitioners — knowledge producers and storytellers themselves — should identify with ways of seeing the world that are at odds with the dominant system, which present challenges to its set of values and hierarchies, and be reassured in the legitimacy of their research work. For those privileged readers whose worldviews and experiences are represented by and through Western technology, the book offers illuminating essays and discussions breaking apart the myth of acultural science and technology.

This book benefits from being composed in the context of the world's oldest living peoples, Australian Aboriginal peoples, with the longest continuum of cultural practice and technologies. In the second part of the book we showcase contemporary Australian Aboriginal digital media projects that continue the creators' cultural practices and storytelling through innovative use of emerging digital technologies.

Equal parts provocation, inspiration, and guide to thinking about and working with emerging digital technologies in a critical way, this publication is intended for a broad audience, from experimental artists to the broader public. Through contributors' case-studies, showcases, and interviews, the collection will challenge 'conventional' thinking on appropriate forms of cultural expression and the apparent neutrality of digital technology. As a whole, the contents form a polemic argument against the characterisation of technology as neutral or acultural, and offers a toolbox of strategies for critical, postcolonial engagement with emerging digital technologies.

WESTERN SCIENCE AND TECHNOLOGY AS COLONIAL CULTURAL PRACTICE

The cultural and historical backdrop to Western science is well documented, yet while it is common from a Western perspective to dismissively frame non-Western systems of knowledge as 'cultural practices', its own approach to making sense of the world, formed out of the specific context of the Enlightenment, is wielded as universal and acultural.

The mythology or 'grand-narrative' of Western scientific rationalism was a tool used to enforce European control over colonies; in one move setting up a system of understanding the world, and using this system as a measure with which to hold itself as superior. It traced human development on a linear scale, with 'enlightened', rational, objective, male Europeans at the apex, and reinforced a system of hierarchy and privilege that placed all others (women, racially 'other' colonial subjects, genderqueer communities) as inferior, weak, and childlike, and used paternalism to justify the invasion and exploitation of others, couched in a sense of moral responsibility (i.e. 'the white man's burden').

As part of these imperial projects, science and colonialism went hand in hand. Explorers like James Cook and botanist Sir Joseph Banks are heroic icons in Australia's colonial history, with their missions to expand imperial territory intertwined with scientific investigation and cartography (e.g. Cook's observance of the transit of venus, Banks' botanical 'discoveries').

Claiming that technology is a cultural practice isn't to say that it rests on the intangible, that western science fails to predict outcomes, or generate utility. It's to say that its way of making sense is contingent on social systems and structures, and is driven by the motivations and 'secular mythologies' of that society.

Satellites orbit the world, relying on an application of the *Theory of Relativity* to correctly provide a GPS position within our *Google Maps* app. The computers we use are able to accomplish an incredibly complex series of tasks to our satisfaction. But these technologies aren't created arbitrarily: they were developed according to the values (economic models, a focus on logistics, and push for bureaucratisation) of powerful interests. In the last hundred years, technologies and scenarios nourished by the dominant, imperial drives of Western society have included Nuclear Weapons[2] (and the concept of Mutual Assured Destruction), Eugenics, and industry unabashedly contributing to Anthropogenic climate change. The GPS we use in our phones is a military technology for strategic maneuvers and accurate targeting; cartography itself (e.g. Great Trigonometrical Survey in India) supported tax collection, policing, and military expansion. The computers we use today are descendents of corporate logistics machines (i.e. *International Business Machines* — IBM), and their development supported by their profitable utilisation for dispassionately tracking and accounting for huge numbers of victims of the Nazi regime.

The direction of technological development isn't a neutral or benign decision – research grants and corporate funding rests on speculation of what will make money (often linked to generous defense funding), and even where a technology has emerged without economic utility, the gap between a proof-of-concept and a utilisable product is often impossible to bridge without finding it a 'market'.

The paradox of Western technoscience is that despite the claim to breath-taking leaps of 'progress', the world is not convincingly better off:

> *At the very point in history where we appear to be able to explain the formation of the universe itself, when we have the ability to utilise energies as great as those of the sun, the majority of the world's population still live in poverty, the resources that made 'modern civilisation' possible are fast being depleted, and the byproducts of that civilisation threaten to transform the climate of the whole world.*[3]

In contrast, technologies developed by Australian Aboriginal peoples have shown their utility to sustainably nurture, nourish, and cultivate the driest inhabited continent on earth for millenia, not only demonstrating the successful stewardship of the environment, but the flourishing of a cultural practice of technology embodying the responsibility to care for Country.

AN OLD, FAMILIAR FUTURE

The future is already here — it's just not very evenly distributed
— William Gibson, science fiction author

In the context of the mid-nineties, rife with techno-utopian dreams of the future, amid the rapid development of the Web as a tool for global knowledge-sharing and the growing sophistication of mobile technologies, Gibson's quote seems like an optimistic herald to an inevitable near-future. But this can be taken a different way — informed by an understanding of the colonial logic resting within the modern practice of technology development we can speculate that this 'uneven distribution' is by design. Not a waiting for everywhere to catch up, for an inevitable even distribution, but actively externalising the costs of modern technology (e.g. in producing the iPhone: child labourers mining Cobalt in DR Congo[4], lakes of pollution in Inner Mongolia[5], suicide-as-protest by Foxconn factory workers[6]) while directing the benefits of empowerment and representation to a small handful of privileged users.

The dynamics of this power inequality are playing out in how contemporary technology is practiced:

Mahli-Ann Butt and Thomas Apperley's paper, *"Shut up and play": Vivian James and the presence of women in gaming cultures,* describes the harassment, and brutal and explicit violence employed by a subset of the male-dominated gamer community to gate-keep participation by women in the digital games community, both as players and creators. These male players feel a sense of ownership over the computer game culture and attempt to regulate the use of technology and prohibit unwanted practices, especially focussing on resisting a push to increase the representation of women and women's stories in games.

Ramsey Nasser's paper, *A Personal Computer for Children of All Cultures,* broadly critiques the aculturality of technology, showing that even at the abstract level of programming languages (effectively tools for building mathematical machines) Western culture and language is inextricably embedded, and that design decisions built on implicit, Anglocentric assumptions has led to programming disadvantaging non-English writers, and practically excluding users of non-roman languages. These sorts of design decisions continue to reproduce inequality through algorithmic bias, and technologies that similarly either disadvantage or entirely exclude, out of a lack of perspective and sense of the universality-of-experience of their creators.

Josh Harle's paper, *Digital Capture: Photogrammetry as rhetoric, fiction, and relic,* examines the use of photogrammetry, a digital scanning technology, for generating and sharing scientific knowledge, arguing that beyond its conformity to conventions of Western science, it is an active form of its continued claim to legitimacy.

Technology does not serve everyone evenly. It ignores some, while others continue to be needed to turn the cogs, to dig up the materials. Benefits are distributed here, damage distributed there. While Western society is happy to fervently embrace the positive aspects of technology, the damage and risk associated with its production is externalised, and hidden from view.

Evident in the progression of modern Western technologies is the drive for power and exploitation. 'Disruptive' technologies actively seek to destabilize labour models and hard-earned protections that were created to redress power imbalances that had existed at least since the Industrial revolution. Social media tools, while seemingly 'free gifts' and occasional tools for community-building and emancipatory participation, subject huge populations of digital subjects to tracking and exploitation as products themselves. Within the iconic technologies of our generation is a continuation of an old story: technologies must serve the powerful, thoroughly engineered to make money and comply to a unifying business logic.

The destructive, exploitative, and unsustainable nature of imperial logic manifested in technology, conceived of as a way of extracting resources,[7] should now be obvious. The world is not an open system, and as much as it may be possible to comfortably ignore the environmental and human costs being exacted in the name of 'progress', it is not possible to ignore the global consequences. Climate change and the migration of dispossessed people are two related crises that offer grave threats to our survival.

While efforts and investment have turned to the production of sustainable technologies, the appearance of sustainability has proven as effective for drawing the interest of consumers, and 'green-washing' has become a marketing activity. Western attempts at sustainable technology has proven problematic, with energy-saving lightbulbs requiring the use of precious metals, and Tesla's endeavours to support renewable energy through battery installations contributing to the rapid depletion of the world's supply of Lithium.

'Decolonising the digital' is not only necessary as a response to the profound inequality of power and representation perpetuated through modern technology, but as an appeal — at a point of crisis — to generate new directions for the forces of science and technology, informed by the full diversity of knowledge systems and voices of the world. What's at stake is the capacity for humanity to understand our world and respond to contemporary challenges, and even grow, in the face of many problems that have been created from the use of Western rationality as a tool for imperialism and inequality.

A WORLD OF DIFFERENT VOICES

By framing the use of technology as a cultural practice, we hope to engage the reader in a critical discussion of how Western 'technoscience' actually operates, who it benefits, and how it can better serve everyone. In destabilising the claim to universality and revealing the Western cultural underpinnings, space is made for the role of diverse knowledges in the task of responding to contemporary challenges.

The supporting myth behind Western science's claim to a single, totalising way of understanding suggests a fundamental inability to believe two different 'sciences' or knowledges could both be legitimate, and through colonial science this has been enacted as a blanket dismissal of non-Western knowledges (as well as local practices deemed as superstitions). However, while Western science is keen to hide its contingency, this mythology falls apart as propaganda when we look at the actual practice of science, through examples such as *Classical Physics* co-existing along-side *Quantum Physics*. One story of the behaviour of masses compliments another. These two 'models' are applied pragmatically to negotiate understanding of the motion of planets, wave-particle duality, or the operation of miniaturized electronics. They are two metaphors, allegories, stories.

As Angie Abdilla's paper, *Beyond Imperial Tools: Future-proofing technology through Indigenous Governance and Traditional Knowledge Systems* suggests, Indigenous peoples' Traditional Knowledges are vitally important in informing the direction of future sustainable and ethical technologies, specifically in areas such as Artificial Intelligence (AI), robotics, Virtual Reality (VR) and Augmented Reality (AR). Within an Indigenous worldview, your sense of place, belonging and purpose in life is firmly grounded and informed by a complex, culturally dynamic science and series of technologies, evolved from a reciprocal relationship with the land, waterways, and skies which have nurtured thousands of generations of Australian Aboriginal peoples.

The Aboriginal and Torres Strait Islander practitioner's works featured in this book showcase the diverse ways in which Indigenous knowledges and innate relationship to the land are able to be continued as new digital cultural practices. The consciousness that exists within Aboriginal Australian technologies old and new — their vitality, resonance, and spirit — are integral for informing a future where Caring for Country and Caring for Kin are the primary motivations of science and technology.

It's our hope that this book encourages and inspires the reader to imagine new practices of technology that are respectful and inclusive of the vast diversity of human experience.

CONTRIBUTIONS

A PERSONAL COMPUTER FOR CHILDREN OF ALL CULTURES

Ramsey Nasser, digital artist

At the time of this writing, the front page of laptop.org is a carousel of beautiful images: children the world over happily toting the colorful OLPC XO laptop. Its moving photos tell the story of the rugged, affordable green-and-white computer produced by the *One Laptop Per Child* project, and the impact it is having on the developing world. Featured are a classroom in Afghanistan, a stairway outside of a home in Nepal, a street in Palestine, and many more such scenes, full of smiling children excitedly using their machines.

Despite the name, OLPC's stated mission is not explicitly to distribute laptops to every child on earth, but rather to "empower the world's poorest children through education." The laptops are a means to this higher, humanitarian end rather than an end in and of themselves. This is by no means new or unique. The vision of the computer as an educational dynamo dates back at least to Seymour Papert's work on Logo at MIT in the late 60s and Alan Kay's work that followed closely after that. By 1972, Kay would produce his seminal paper *A Personal Computer for Children of All Ages*, which described the then- and still-hypothetical *Dynabook* computer. While mostly famous for inspiring the form factors of modern laptops and tablets, the paper is also significant in that it explicitly frames the Dynabook and computer programming as tools for "learning by making". The first speculative story Kay includes involves youngsters Beth and Jimmy learning about gravitational physics by playing and reprogramming a video game. Unsurprisingly, Kay and Papert were both involved in the launch of the OLPC project in 2005, bookending their careers as pioneers of educational computing. As the world becomes more digital, and computer literacy becomes important for participation in society and the workforce, the image of the computer as a universal engine of education and empowerment—almost as old as computing itself—has only become more pronounced.

More than most computer projects, the OLPC XO takes "localization" seriously. In pursuit of the project's global goals the interface of their operating system and its documentation are available in a variety of world languages. Digging past the surface, however, one finds that the provided programming experience is built on the popular *Python* programming language, notably made up of English language words and for which no localization is provided. Furthermore, the XO provides a terminal program to access the underlying UNIX system and, in the words of the project, "[allow] kids to dig deeper into their systems, issue commands, and make modifications to their laptops." But a UNIX terminal interacts with utilities from the POSIX standard, all of which have English language names, and for which no localization is provided. The dependency of parts of the XO on a particular written language seems to fly in the face of the goals of the project, so why is it there at all?

The fictional Dynabook is presented as an abstract, neutral platform for its users to engage with and repurpose. But the production of OLPC XO reveals the crucial difference between an idealized computer and a real one: real computers are technical artifacts produced by thousands of engineers over hundreds of person-years of labor. They are the accumulation of countless software and hardware components made by people who never directly coordinated with one another in most cases, and whose work is likely being used in manners increasingly divergent from any of their original intentions. Every one of these components necessarily makes assumptions about itself, how it will be used, and the world in which it will exist.

Adopting UNIX and Python were certainly pragmatic and effective design decisions for the XO. But those technologies and others turn out to have deeply rooted assumptions around the English language that the OLPC project cannot meaningfully alter, and the result is that if any of the smiling children from Afghanistan, Nepal, or Palestine were curious enough to pull back the layers of their laptops, they would invariably encounter a language foreign to them. Could OLPC have made different decisions? If the humanitarian project poised to empower the world's poorest children produces machines that carry a bias for a particular written culture, what other fields of computing do the same? Does it matter? How empowering can a computing experience in another language be? And is an entirely non-English computing experience even possible?

VISIBLE BIAS

Another corner of computing exhibiting a surprising and highly visible linguistic bias is digital typography. Many production-grade typesetting systems use a simple text-layout algorithm that works something like this: given a font and text to display, for each character of the text:

1. Look up the character's glyph in the font
2. Display the glyph on the screen
3. Move the cursor to the right by the width of the glyph

This approach is used in high profile projects including *ImGui*[1] and *Three.js*[2], and it effectively bakes in the assumptions that every character has exactly one corresponding glyph, and that text flows in a single direction. These assumptions are simple to implement and suit the Latin script that these systems were designed for, but fail for other languages. The Arabic script in particular presents something of a worst-case scenario: unlike Latin, Arabic flows from right-to-left and in certain circumstances glyphs are positioned vertically, and unlike Latin, Arabic is always cursive, meaning the same letter will have a different glyph depending on its surrounding letters. Other scripts like Devanagari and Thai are similarly poorly served and cannot be rendered correctly without considerable additional work.

This contributes to the consistent public butchering of non-Latin text by digital typesetting software. I maintain a blog at nopenotarabic.tumblr.com to keep track of examples of these issues as they affect the Arabic script. Examples of highly visible rendering failures include the Athens Airport, Pokemon Go, a Lil Uzi Vert video, Coke ads, Pepsi ads, Google ads, Captain America: Civil War, and anti-Trump art, among others (see Figures 1 and 2).

The Arabic in each example exhibits the exact same error: the text is correctly spelled but rendered backwards (i.e. from left-to-right), and none of the letters are joined. The resulting text does not approach legibility and may as well be chicken scratch to an Arabic reader. What's most likely happening in every one of these cases is that well-meaning but non-Arabic-speaking graphic designers are pasting Arabic language text into their graphics packages which is not equipped for it, and, seeing something vaguely Arabic-looking with no error message, considering their job done and moving on.

The experience of seeing text like this in public is a deeply hurtful reminder to every Arabic reader that the digital world was not built for them, and that their culture is an afterthought at best. Seeing text like this in an otherwise high budget movie or video game is its own kind of cultural violence, making a mockery of a script that is native and even holy to many. It is a communication by non-Arabs for non-Arabs, and it reveals a willingness to use Arabic as a cultural prop, but none to do the work to get it right.

TECHNOLOGY AS CULTURAL PRACTICE

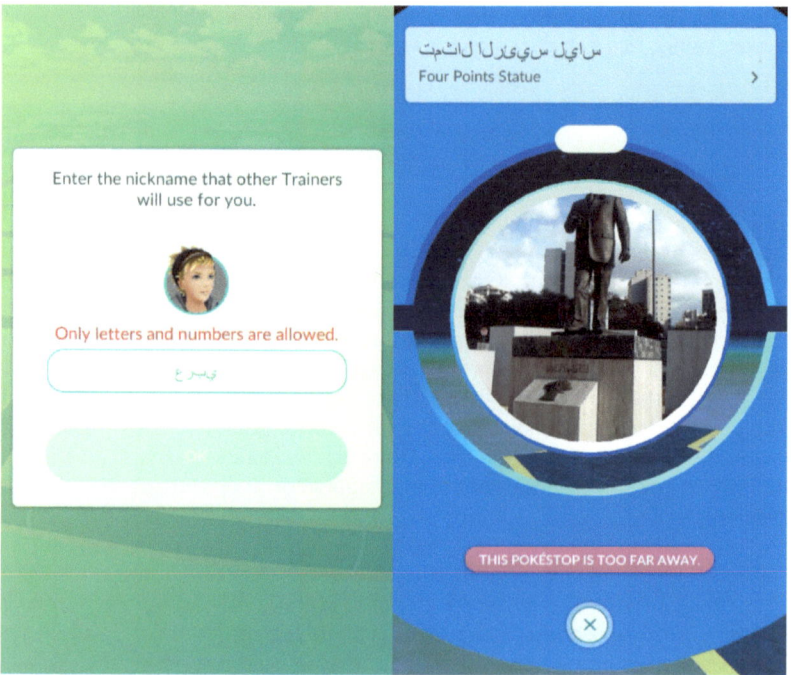

Figure 1

These failures happen in two places. First off, they're evidence of a lack of diversity in production and graphic design firms. Had there been Arabs or Persians or Pakistanis present in the design or decision-making process or even consulted as subject matter experts these mistakes would have been caught immediately and most likely addressed. I can speak from personal experience and say I know that my presence as an Arab on or adjacent to software projects allowed me to point out incorrect rendering and prevent butchered script from going public on more than one occasion.

Second, the tools that are commonly available and claim to handle "text" have failed because instead of actually handling all text, they were really only designed and tested for the Latin alphabet. Instead of issuing a warning when faced with non-Latin text they did not support, they displayed a butchered version of the script that was similar enough to the real thing to fool the designers in charge. Adobe products before the Creative Cloud era and major game engines like Unity 3D and Unreal are all guilty of this. Technical solutions exist, but engineers have been slow to update large legacy codebases, and the problem persists.

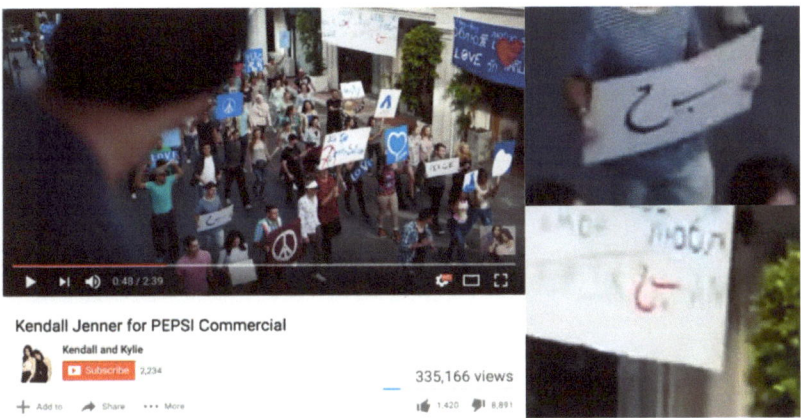

Figure 2

INVISIBLE BIAS

Although errors in text rendering get splashed across the billboards and screens of the world, bias towards the English language is deepest in the less visible world of computer programming languages. And while text rendering is slowly getting better, the situation is much more bleak in the world of programming, where it is much harder to find a toehold for hope.

Every programming language in serious use today is based on words and punctuation taken from the English language and writing conventions. In order to use these tools, some knowledge of English is a requirement. In order to use these tools most effectively, actual proficiency in English is unavoidable. This favors programmers natively familiar with English over others and makes a truly inclusive and culturally neutral programming experience impossible.

As concrete examples, consider these three recursive implementations of the Fibonacci sequence in Python, Swift and Ruby taken from the Rosettacode project:

Python

```python
def fibRec(n):
  if n < 2:
    return n
  else:
    return fibRec(n-1) + fibRec(n-2)
```

Swift

```swift
func fibonacci(n: Int) -> Int {
  if n < 2 {
    return n
  } else {
    return fibonacci(n-1) + fibonacci(n-2)
  }
}
```

Ruby

```ruby
def fib(n, sequence=[1])
 n.times do
  current_number, last_number = sequence.last(2)
  sequence << current_number + (last_number or 0)
 end
 sequence.last
end
```

These languages are useful as specimens of the dominant family of programming languages as of the time of this writing, but the following critique will apply to every language in contemporary use. Full and abbreviated English language words abound, and they can broadly be separated into two categories: keywords and identifiers.

Most languages provide some set of basic built-in functionality that is not subject to creation or modification by the user. Syntax for this functionality is provided via keywords, parts of the language that are "baked in" and receive special treatment by the interpreter or compiler. Examples of these in the above examples are **def** in Ruby and Python (short for "define") and **func** in Swift (short for "function") which introduce new functions. **if** and **else** in Python and Swift denote conditional branches to control the flow of program execution. **return** in Python and Swift cause a function to terminate and produce a result. Finally, while Python uses indentation to denote the start and end of its blocks of code and Swift uses curly braces, Ruby uses the English word **end** to mark the end of a block started by a **def** or a **do** keyword.

Identifiers are names that the programmer assigns to functions, values, and data structures. It is up to the programmer to define them, though the language will impose restrictions on what constitutes a legal identifier. In these examples, each function is given a name **fibRec** (short for "fibonacci recursive"), **fibonacci**, and **fib**, by the programmer. In theory they could be anything, though the chosen names convey the intent of the functions well. A bit trickier are the identifiers **last**, **times**, and **println**. These are names of functions that are provided by the standard library of the language, a set of useful utilities included with the language itself that allows programmers to be productive right away without having to reinvent standard operations. They are technically not treated differently from a programmer's own functions, and in theory could be replaced, though in practice this can be a challenge and is generally not done.

This distinction is important because it separates the English language content of modern code into two categories: one which is an intrinsic part of the programming language itself and one which is at least in theory subject to change from the outside. At first glance, the former category seems to be the more entrenched one, requiring entirely new languages to be designed to introduce new keywords. That was my first intuition, but with time I came to find that the latter category, the one of user-defined names, is the insurmountable challenge that makes large scale non-English programming impossible.

قلب: لغة برمجة

Despite growing up in Lebanon speaking Arabic and studying Computer Science in Beirut, none of this was immediately obvious to me. I had the privilege of being proficient in English for most of my life, so I never gave much thought to the fact that every programming language I had ever seen shared a common linguistic heritage. When I moved to New York for graduate school my research took me towards designing better languages for new programmers. Initially my focus was on moving away from the old syntaxes and semantics of the 70s and towards something more modern. But with time I realized that every design for a new language I conceived of used English language words pervasively. The English-centric assumptions ran deep enough to color not only my present, but also my imagination for different futures. I started to wonder who were these "new programmers" for whom I was designing, and what was the effect of the natural language their programming experience was based on.

To probe this question and confront my own biases I became interested in designing a non-English programming language for non-English speaking new programmers. I picked Arabic as it is my native language and what I know best, and I knew that I had to make a new language in order to get away from the English keywords baked into all existing languages.

The language I built was called قلب, pronounced qalb or 'alb in the Lebanese dialect that I speak. The word means "heart" and is a recursive acronym for :قلب لغة برمجة, pronounced 'alb: lughat barmajeh, meaning "heart: a programming language." This is what the Fibonacci function from above looks like.

(حدد فيبوناتشي (لامدا (ن)

(إذا (أصغر؟ ن ٢)

ن

(جمع (فيبوناتشي (طرح ن ١))

(فيبوناتشي (طرح ن ٢))))))

With support from the Eyebeam Art and Technology Center, I developed the قلب interpreter towards the end of 2012. It was crucially important that قلب not be a speculative project, but a real functioning programming language. I wanted to go as far as I could following all the rules of classic language design and implementation to understand why deviating from English never happens in practice.

قلب is, by design, a boring programming language. It is a text-book Scheme interpreter based on Peter Norvig's *Lispy*—the kind a first year Computer Science student might turn in for an assignment. Its sole deviation from Norvig's interpreter is in using a non-English language with a non-Latin script as its basis, treating the rest of the language as the control in the experiment.

In some ways قلب succeeds in providing a non-English programming experience. First off, it provides Arabic keywords in place of the more ubiquitous English ones. **if** becomes إذا, **def** becomes حدد, and even mathematical operators like + and - are written out as Arabic words جمع and طرح. Furthermore, the parser will reject user supplied identifiers that contain anything but Arabic letters, effectively requiring every visible word in the language to be in Arabic. And with the Arabic numerals used in Latin languages replaced with the Indic digits more common in Arabic, قلب's rejection of English is complete.

TECHNOLOGY AS CULTURAL PRACTICE

This small change is enough to cause serious problems, however. The project's source code is hosted at github.com/nasser/--- rather than the more correct github.com/nasser/قلب because GitHub requires ASCII-only project names, and collapses non-ASCII characters into hyphens. Text editors are easily confused by Arabic script, often failing to correctly remap the arrow keys and displaying source code in a manner reminiscent of the nopenotarabic blog. Similarly, terminal emulators used to interact with command line tools can be stumped by the presence of Arabic text. These failings and more make the act of programming in قلب tedious and error-prone compared to programming in the better supported English based languages. By choosing a language other than English as its basis, قلب reveals hidden linguistic biases in programming tools that otherwise "just work." It is not a language a programmer could ever be comfortable or productive in as a result.

These frustrations alone are not enough to doom the whole project, however. With time and effort, better text editors and terminal emulators can be written, and the assumptions that web hosting platforms make can be revised. What makes قلب or any project like it impossible to succeed at scale rather than merely difficult is something much deeper, and ultimately, much less technical.

THE OBJECTIVE BECOMES SUBJECTIVE

Computers are fundamentally number processing machines. As a piece of physical hardware a CPU is really only capable of basic operations on numeric data, like arithmetic, loading numbers from memory, and writing numbers to memory. When people point out that computers are "just ones and zeroes" this is likely what they are referring to: the binary representation of numbers that a computer manipulates. This is the closest computers come to being truly neutral devices.

The problem is that people generally want their computers to be more than giant calculators. Early computers were just that: engines to compute bomb trajectories and crack enemy encryption during war. But as the decades passed and they became more widely available and integrated into people's lives their tasks grew while their fundamental architecture remained largely unchanged. Modern computers seem to handle a lot more than numbers, from text to images to audio and video, but all of that data is still represented numerically at the level of the machine. And while numbers do have a measure of objectivity to them, the manner in which non-numerical data is represented numerically is completely subjective.

Representing Writing

Take text, for example. Text can be represented digitally as a sequence of numbers by assigning a number to each character in a natural language. The crucial question is: which numbers should represent which characters? Pure mathematics has nothing to say here because the mapping is arbitrary. It does not matter as long as it's consistent. If you decide that 0 should be 'A' and 1 should be 'B' and so on, you've successfully represented text as numbers. In an isolated context, there's little more to it than that. But as software is confronted with other software it is forced to communicate, and if everyone invents their own digital representation of text, their programs will not be able to share textual data. If a program designed using the above mentioned representation received text from a program that decided that 0 should in fact represent 'Z' and 1 should represent 'Y' and so on, it would misinterpret the data. In this case, neither program would have done anything technically wrong, but the failure rather would have come from the human programmers' lack of agreement.

This level of coordination is crucially important for the interoperation of computer systems. Historically, national standards bodies would define text encodings for a nation's computer systems to use. With the advent of the internet, even this approach became insufficient, as software had to deal with textual data from other nations. The Unicode Consortium was formed in 1991 to define a single encoding for all human writing systems: the *Unicode Encoding*. At its heart, the Unicode Encoding is an enormous table mapping numbers to characters in different scripts that almost every computing system in use has agreed upon. This allows text to be processed by computers as numbers, but the subjective meaning of those numbers comes this international agreement negotiated far and away from inside a CPU.

It is through assigning meaning to numbers that human bias and history too creeps into software. And Unicode itself is far from perfect. For example, for historical reasons Latin characters are assigned the lowest numbers and as a result can take up less space in memory than characters in other languages. To preserve space in the encoding, Han characters "common" to Chinese, Japanese, and Korean are assigned the same number, making distinguishing national variants difficult in some cases, and hurting Unicode's popularity in East Asia. There is consistent debate around new writing systems, and the decision around what language gets added to the standard is a deeply human, deeply political one.

The Second Hard Problem In Computer Science

Computer programming is an exercise in managing enormous amounts of complexity. The stream of millions if not billions of binary numbers needed to execute a non-trivial program at the level of a CPU immediately dwarfs the human mind. In order to make sense of anything within a finite lifespan, programmers use programming languages to act as a layer between themselves and the machine that will run their code. Their programming languages present a suite of tools more palatable to human thinking to express programs that will eventually be turned into streams of numbers a computer expects. One of the most prevalent and powerful of these tools is the ability to name things.

Assigning a name to a procedure or data structure makes it easier to think about and reuse. Compare reasoning about "the function at address 9036724" to "the print function", or "the value at offset 24" to "the 'name' field of the 'Person' record." Programming languages perform this transformation when compiling a programmer's code into machine code, and in general the particulars of this process can safely be regarded as an implementation detail and paid no mind. Programmers as a result are given this convenient abstraction to work within, where code and data can have meaningful names, and the computer can continue to process numbers as it always has.

Names also facilitate a crucial kind of collaboration in software. Programmers often share useful code they have written as *libraries*, also known as *frameworks* or *software development kits* in some contexts. By learning the names of the procedures and data structures in a library other programmers can build on the work of the original authors and avoid redundant effort. Libraries also provide mechanisms for a programmer's code to talk to an operating system or hardware, like Apple's *iOS Software Development Kit*, or IEEE's POSIX standard.

It is important to stress that modern programming is only possible because of this collaboration. A programmer today is only able to write an application "from scratch" in less time than ever before because they are building on decades of existing code written by programmers they've never met, published as libraries. Without sharing code, every programming endeavor would have to start from the level of the hardware every time, and progress that transcends an individual project would be impossible.

Another important detail is that procedures and data structures in libraries must be accessed by way of the names they were assigned by their original author. These names fall in the category of identifiers discussed earlier. They are subject to definition by the original programmer of a library, and in theory could be anything the language considers a legal identifier. But a user of a library must include the exact names chosen by the original author in their own code and cannot exchange them for anything else. Put another way, the names used in libraries are not merely decorative or explanatory, they are an essential part of the library itself. Even more, the wider the use a library finds the more incentive there is to never change any of its names, as that would require rewriting any code that used the old names, and the amount of labor involved could be intractable. For example, consider the function **malloc** from the POSIX standard. **malloc** is a standard way for a program to request memory from an operating system. The name is cryptic to new programmers, but it is short for "memory allocate" and contractions like that were popular in the programming of decades past. But changing **malloc** to, say, the arguably more readable **memoryAllocate** is impossible as it would require the billions of lines of code deployed around the world already referring to **malloc** to be updated.

This inertia extends beyond libraries and into protocols, another realm of software coordination. Protocols are agreements between programmers on the formatting of data so that software systems can communicate. Many of them have no linguistic properties, only specifying the order of bytes numerically. But some so-called "readable" protocols do encode data as language, and are subject to the same problems as libraries. An example is the RFC 2616 specifying the *Hypertext Transfer Protocol*, HTTP or more commonly "the Web." HTTP uses named "headers" as part of the communication between a server and a browser. Each header has a name and a value. Examples of header names include **Location, Retry-After, Last-Modified**, and **If-Modified-Since**. A system participating in HTTP as a server or browser must use these exact headers with their punctuation, spelling and capitalization or it will be ignored for generating invalid data. Like libraries, these names are a hard requirement of the protocol, and no substitution is possible without creating a new protocol. As one of the most widely distributed protocols on earth, these names are practically eternal, to the point that even spelling mistakes in the original specification cannot be changed anymore. One of the HTTP headers is **Referer**, missing an r, but fixing that typo in every server and browser on the planet would likely be prohibitively expensive at this point.

Indeed names are so important that Kay's description for the programming language of the Dynabook revolves almost exclusively around them

> *The use of this language is essentially divided into two activities: 1. giving names to objects and classes (memory association), and 2. retrieving objects and classes by supplying the name under which they had been previously stored. A process consists of these (activities) and is terminated when there are no longer any names under scrutiny.*

Although all of such a language can be easily derived from just these two notions, a few names would have an a priori meaning in order to allow interesting things to be done right away.

And Computer Scientist Phil Karlton's famous joke uses them as a punchline:

There are only two hard things in Computer Science: cache invalidation and naming things.

Naming things *is* terribly important and difficult, but not for the reasons most Computer Science texts get into. Absent from most conversations about names in programming is how deeply cultural the act of naming something is. Historically, naming a territory was part of the spoils of war, attested to by dozens of cities named "Alexandria" from Egypt to Afghanistan left behind by Alexander the Great's global conquest. Names attributed to a thing also encode the perspectives of the namer. What Westerners refer to as China is known to its indigenous population as *Zhōngguó*, meaning "Central Kingdom." The name China likely comes from the Sanskrit or Persian names for the long-passed *Qin* dynasty. My own personal name, Ramsey, was deliberately chosen by my parents to be pronounceable in the West and in my native Lebanon (رمزي, *Remzi*, in Arabic) as they imagined my future before I was even born. Naming is a deeply human act that records history and language and can be poetic, beautiful, violent, and just about anything but neutral.

And therein lies the problem. Names are what allow human minds to comprehend and manipulate the vast complexity of computing, and modern programming is only made possible by building on existing systems. This necessitates using protocols and libraries built by others and invoking names of their choosing in any new code. As there is no such thing as a culturally neutral name, programmers today are forced into familiarity with the written culture of programmers past. The earlier examples from POSIX and HTTP had their roots in the English language that their authors were fluent in, and this is true of every library and protocol in contemporary use. Programming is always a social and collaborative act. Even when one is working alone, a programmer is always indirectly collaborating with the thousands of programmers that came before them and adapting the systems they left behind to new uses. The progress made at American organizations like Bell Labs and Xerox PARC from the 60s onward gave us the foundations of modern software, but also enshrined the culture of those engineers into every programming system that followed.

The fact that using English language names is unavoidable when interacting with libraries and protocols is what makes قلب, and any project like it, ultimately doomed to failure. Non-English programming projects are confronted with an impossible choice: cling to your conceptual and political purity and be cut off from the world of software, or abandon purity, allow English identifiers, and defeat your own purpose for existing. قلب itself is only able to implement basic games and browser interactions by maintaining a bridge between itself and JavaScript code internally, though this is effectively a cheat, and there is no way to expose this mechanism to the programmer. Purely non-English languages could never talk to the web, or email, or any other protocol based on English language. They could not build on the sixty years of software libraries written using English names, and would have to reinvent it all from scratch themselves, siloing them off from the rest of the world and from history, which is both unrealistic and undesirable.

The reality is that programming will most likely remain dominated by English indefinitely, and familiarity with the language is a prerequisite for entrance into the software engineering industry. A true Computer For Children of All Cultures, a computing experience where a learner could pull back layer after layer of software and never encounter anything but their own written culture is not meaningfully possible unless their written culture happens to be American English. When I think about قلب and the possibility of a young Arab learning how to program in their own language, only to inevitably outgrow the limitations of the system and eventually realize that to become a "real" programmer they'd have to learn English after all, it breaks my heart. That isn't a moment I want to craft for anyone, and why I consider قلب an impossible project. The door to a non-English programming experience is closed now, if it was ever open, and as time passes and more software gets written, it closes tighter still.

THE DIFFICULT PROBLEMS ARE NEVER THE TECHNICAL ONES

Accepting that the problem is not technical or computer-specific, but cultural and linguistic is a step towards imagining different futures. The central question is not "how do we build non-English programming experiences?" but rather the much trickier "how do we facilitate communication across linguistic boundaries?" A definitive answer is difficult, but there are a few non-solutions that can be discarded right away.

First off, projects like قلب that attempt to do what English-based programming does but in another language are not the way forward. As demonstrated above, the deep reliance on named things in programming reveals a flaw in the premise of such projects. But even if they could be overcome, investing an enormous amount of effort to add a single language to the pantheon of programming is beside the point. At best, it gets us towards A Personal Computer For Children of Some Cultures—whichever cultures can afford to invest in reinventing the history of software engineering—which is a much less compelling goal. Recreating existing power structures with a different group on top is not an act of liberation.

Picking a "common" auxiliary language on which to build programming languages on is also likely a dead end, primarily because such a language does not exist. *Esperanto* gets framed as such, but its script and grammatical structure are decidedly European and hardly global. A true auxiliary language for the people of the world that would be appropriate to consider as the foundation for a future of programming would borrow much more from Chinese, Hindi, and Arabic. The absence of such a language and the difficulty in designing and popularizing one makes this a poor way forward as well.

Finally, the more pragmatic-minded might suggest a system that involves automatically translating identifiers from the English-based ecosystem to the languages of the world. It's important to reject this on both technical and political grounds. Technically, machine translation is poor to the point of being unusable in most cases, and programming is full of made up words. For example, what is the Pashto translation of **AbstractSingletonProxyFactoryBean**[3]? The technical shortcomings reveal the political problems: a translation based approach makes non-English languages second class citizens of the programming world. "Real" programming would continue to be done in English, while translations were generated for everyone else, modulo quality of translation. Again, this isn't true equity, and not a terribly exciting goal to work towards.

None of these approaches meaningfully begin to build the bridge across the linguistic gap between human beings that would be required for a truly equitable programming experience. Ideally, the languages of the world could pool together and build on each other. Code written in Arabic could use code written in French, which could build on code written in Japanese. With no specific natural language receiving special treatment, all languages could be treated equally, and a new common programming experience could emerge from it all.

This is a fantasy, but there have been moments in the human history where common languages emerged out of necessity. From the 11th to the 19th century sailors and traders around the Mediterranean spoke a language called *sabir* or *lingua franca*, an organic blend of Italian, Spanish, Portuguese, Berber, Arabic, Turkish, and Greek. This language was not designed but rather emerged naturally from the interactions of merchants from different cultures trying to do their jobs. Though far from equitable or utopian, it was a situation where one side could not easily assert complete linguistic dominance over any other, resulting in an emergent new means of communicating.

What would a *lingua franca* for programming look like? How does one design a programming language to emerge naturally from its users as opposed to being passed down unchanged from the past? It is hard to say. Such a language would face all the challenges mentioned here, and be incompatible with most current internet protocols and software ecosystems. But if it could promise a truly equitable programming experience upon which to build a real Personal Computer For Children Of All Cultures, it *just might* be worth hitting the reset button.

TECHNOLOGY AS CULTURAL PRACTICE

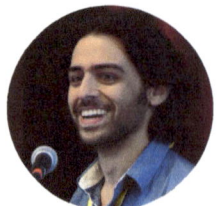

Ramsey Nasser is a computer scientist, game designer, and educator based in Brooklyn. He researches programming languages by building tools to make computing more expressive and makes work that questions the basic assumptions we make about code itself. His games playfully push people out of their comfort zones, and are often built using experimental tools of his design. Ramsey is a former Eyebeam fellow and a professor at schools around New York.

"SHUT UP AND PLAY":
VIVIAN JAMES AND THE PRESENCE OF WOMEN IN GAMING CULTURES

Mahli-Ann Rakkomkaew Butt, The University of Sydney
Thomas Apperley, Tampere University, Finland

Content warning: This paper contains discussion of sexual violence.

INTRODUCTION

A widely adopted fallacy is that the internet creates an inherently egalitarian utopia for online communication and communities. One consequence of this fallacy is that online interactions are considered gender-neutral, and that questions of gender equity in online communities are irrelevant. Conversely, early digital theorist Sean Cubitt has argued that a characteristic of online cultures is the rapid importation and re-inscription of pre-existing hierarchies.[1] In the case of videogames, notions of masculinity quickly became predominant in early gaming cultures in both the USA[2] and the UK[3]. The form of masculinity that was developed was in opposition to dominant forms of masculinity,[4] creating a culture of the underdog where gamers were united against threats to their hobby from those 'outsiders' that did not 'get' videogames. This chapter addresses how recent controversies, namely *#gamergate*, have highlighted the need for gaming cultures to escape this highly limiting 'us' and 'them' model. This mindset of ownership and exclusion, and the dominance of a particular culture of use and creation is a key area of digital culture that demands interrogation, as it limits the possibilities of games as a medium, and the impact of the technology as a medium for education, development, and diverse expression, because it can only include women and girls on the strictest behavioural caveats. The inclusion of women is based on an implied presupposition that they accept the heteronormative and male dominated status quo.

This chapter examines the sexism and misogyny embedded in #gamergate through a case study of the figure of Vivian James. Vivian James is a crowd-sourced game avatar, who also appears as a fictional character in several genres of communication, mostly widely in fan art. Through a visual analysis of Vivian James, this chapter marks out the everydayness of the normative policing that is championed by #gamergate, which is underwritten by the threat of sexual violence. We will begin by providing a brief introduction to #gamergate, before moving to more detailed analysis of Vivian James herself, and how she represents the constant threat of violence for outspoken women in gaming cultures.

#GAMERGATE

The events which constituted #gamergate were an intensification of the hostility towards women which was already an unfortunate element in gaming cultures. The events which occurred and the aftermath need to be contextualised against a long history of anti-women activities within this predominantly masculine hobby. Since the advent of smartphones and the emergence of popular and influential social and mobile games in the past decade, gaming cultures have been increasingly opened to women. The games industry has come to understand the importance of women as consumers, and more women have been encouraged to join the games industry as designers, developers and critics. Although gender parity is yet to be achieved these changes were viewed largely as positive steps by players and the games industry. However scholars also noted that this new inclusion of women in games culture as game players, developers and tastemakers was on particular terms. The "new gaming public" which included women, was quick to exclude any women who were critical of gaming culture, particularly those who spoke out against sexism in game cultures and the games industry.[5] As women like Zoë Quinn, Anita Sarkeesian, and Brianna Wu became more prominent and included in the industry, and influential in gaming cultures through crowd-funding their own projects, some male gamers saw their presence as an attack on games and gamers themselves. Sarkeesian's work as a critic of the games industry was singled out at first as she was particularly critical of how the game industry portrayed women in games.

However, it was a specific event which precipitated the intensification of anti-woman sentiment, which quickly became known as #gamergate. This started with the deliberate and public 'slut-shaming' of Zoë Quinn, a game developer famous for the innovative empathy game *Depression Quest*. At 12:42 a.m. on 16th August, 2014, her ex-boyfriend posted a 9,425-word blog post—titled "The Zoë Post"—about their relationship.[6] Methodically designed to inflict the most personal and professional damage on Quinn, the post was quickly shared and discussed on social media, particularly on 4Chan forums, which were notorious for coordinating anti-woman harassment.[7] The wide circulation of "The Zoë Post" prompted anonymous users to begin conspiring to coordinate attacks against Quinn in IRC chat rooms.[8] It was seen as evidence of a widespread feminist conspiracy behind the recent progressive shifts in gaming that were being pushed from outsiders to gaming culture.[9] This triggered outrage and a demand for coordinated retaliation against the infiltration of 'political correctness' that was dictated by feminists and their supporters who did not 'get' gaming culture. Angry gamers, incited by "The Zoë Post," and conspiratorial commentaries began to target other high-profile women in the games industry including developer Brianna Wu, and game critic Anita Sarkeesian. The criminal acts that were documented during the harassment campaign included doxxing,[10] swatting,[11] death threats, rape threats, bomb threats, and a university massacre threat.[12] These life-threatening crimes against prominent women in games created a hostile environment for women gamers more generally, as it highlighted the precarity of their inclusion in gaming culture and vulnerability to harassment and further, more serious, crimes.

A key issue for people that supported these attacks was the notion that "The Zoë Post" revealed a conspiracy by left-leaning and feminist game journalists and critics to force change in the games industry. By August 27, conservative actor Adam Baldwin had coined the hashtag "#GamerGate" to reference the so-called scandal.[13] The perceived collective of outsider feminists and their supporters were disparagingly dubbed "Social Justice Warriors."[14] While many parties actively involved in the #gamergate harassment of women presented themselves as motivated by a demand for ethics in game journalism, scholarly consensus has found that, rather than a cohesive movement calling for ethical practices, #gamergate is a decentralized harassment campaign that prevents women from working in the games industry and enjoying gaming as a pastime.[15] This harassment creates an overarching climate of hostility and fear in the community, especially among women and other marginalized groups.[16]

The emergence of #gamergate merely reflects a wider problem of systemic sexism pervasive in the games industry and gaming cultures. Early gaming cultures were largely male dominated, and over time sexism and misogyny have been normalized to be almost unremarkable. The events of #gamergate is one of various anti-feminist guideposts throughout an already extensive history of harassment towards women[17] and hegemonic masculinity[18] that shapes the everyday experiences of female players, and convinces many potential players that gaming is 'not for them'. For some gamers, gaming and game cultures had become a space where they could continue to escape from mainstream masculinity,[19] such as sports, while still enacting "their private, escapist power fantasies."[20] In game cultures, young men could embrace their underdog status, while also ignoring the progressive politics which had impacted to a greater or lesser degree on almost every other element of public life. One of the key challenges for activists and scholars in the wake of #gamergate is to recontextualize the 'naturalness' of gaming as a male-dominated sphere. Destabilizing the hierarchical and binary thinking of "us" (traditional demographic of male gamers) and "them" (effectively anyone else — newer female gamers, but also non-white and genderqueer gamers) supports the diversification of gaming culture by opening it to multifarious participation.

CONFIGURING VIVIAN JAMES

The figure of Vivian James is an important one for #gamergate because it demonstrates the forms of inclusion that they believe are appropriate for women in gaming culture. In the wake of the controversy it offers an important perspective on the pervasive anti-woman attitudes in game cultures which drove the events. To recognise that the operation of sexism in these spaces can be both brutal and opaque, and subtle and insidious. Vivian James demonstrates the everyday and mundane sexism that is pervasive in some elements of gaming culture, and impacts on the everyday experiences of women gamers and women in the games industry.

The character, figure, and avatar of Vivian James was originally conceived as a crowdsourced avatar for the game *Afterlife Empire*,[21] with her appearance collective configured in order to signal a fantasy of inclusivity, which clearly embodies deeply problematic notions of the place of women in gaming culture. The crowdfunding for Vivian James began shortly after the circulation of "The Zoë Post." A collective of anonymous 4Chan users on /v/ forum decided to sponsor a Toronto based organization *The Fine Young Capitalists* (TFYC) through their crowdfunding campaign in the IndieGoGo platform. TFYC were running a competition supporting women game designers with the proceeds going to charity, and backers of the IndieGoGo campaign were allowed to choose which charity would receive their donation. As part of the highest tier of sponsorship (those who donated $2,000 USD, or more) the donors could submit an avatar design that would be included in the game. Mobilized through the /v/ forum, the pro-#gamergate 4Chan users became the highest contributors to TFYC, raising over $23,000 USD.[22] As a result the avatar that they collectively designed, Vivian James, was included in *Afterlife Empire*.

The group that funded *Afterlife Empire* and designed Vivian James only did so as an expression of solidarity with #gamergate. The /v/ forum supported the IndieGoGo campaign to spite Zoë Quinn, who had publicly disagreed with TFYC earlier in 2014 about the underpayment and exploitation of their female employees.[23] The fundraising project was called "Operation Chemo Butthurt," a reference to how part of their proceeds were donated to The Colon Cancer Alliance.[24] The reference to 'butthurt' in the project had a double meaning, it is both a potentially offensive way of referring to colon cancer, and also in subcultural parlance, slang for someone who is easily, or needlessly offended by perceived slights and insults. The naming of "Operation Chemo Butthurt" follows a common pattern of 'edgy' behavior and language among sexist and misogynist gamers: a deliberate provocation of 'offensiveness' that is a tasteless and unsubtle, even forced joke that contrives a barrier against accountability.

The design concept that the 4chan /v/ forum put forward for Vivian James as a representative of #gamergate in *Afterlife Empire* (see Figure 1), describes her as:

> *Just an average female gamer to troll everyone... ...All the tards in the media will expect some sort of pedocrap or LOLSORANDOM shit and we will just give them a simple average girl.*[25]

Consistent throughout the conceptualization of Vivian James was a logic that, by virtue of the designed avatar possessing female qualities, it could not be seen as sexist. The assumption among the funders and supporters of the IndieGoGo campaign, was that a combination of their support for the TFYC women in games competition, together with the design of Vivian James herself would reform the sexist and misogynist reputation that #gamergate supporters had aptly acquired through media coverage.

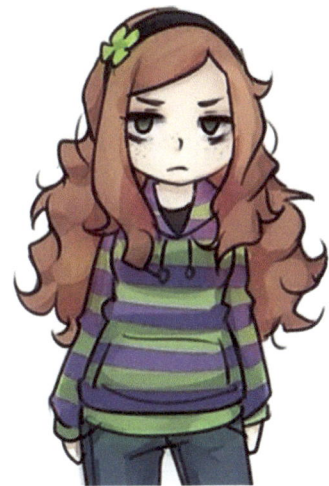

Figure 1

Vivian James emerged from an ad hoc collection of individuals who believed that it was appropriate to harass female game developers, and who also thought that they needed to suggest a more inclusive image for #gamergate in order to avoid bad press. The submission to TFYC describes Vivian James's personality in a way which reflected their attitude towards inclusion: "Tough-loves video games; Loathes dishonesty and hypocrisy; Low-affect, grumpy, perpetually fed up and tired."[26] She isn't emotional ("low-affect"), values ethics in journalism ("loathes dishonesty and hypocrisy") and importantly actually loves videogames, maybe a bit too much because they are keeping her up at night ("tough-love"; "perpetually...tired").

This particular construction of women gamers acquired a very telling unofficial tagline: "shut up and play." Her personality and attributes were further developed through various iterations by fan-artists,[27] which were shared and commented on in numerous gaming forums. Her personality was whittled down to describing her as *a girl who just wants to play videogames*: "[s]he doesn't care about rights, agenda, or how you feel [...] she will only speak with you if you grab the controller and play."[28] In this respect, Vivian James exemplifies how #gamergate wants women to 'shut up' about their negative experiences of gaming,[29] and the precarious inclusion that women have in the new gaming public.[30] The construction and expression of Vivian James thus provide scope for understanding and unpacking how deeply some men are invested in the forceful protection of what they perceive as 'their' territory.

SILENCING AND VIOLENCE

Vivian James is inextricably tied to toxic male cultures attempting to control the public perception of #gamergate, and policing female 'intrusion' into digital games and gaming cultures. The carefully designed appearance and one-sided persona of Vivian James promotes a mode of inclusion for women in gaming and game cultures that demands nothing short of the silent acceptance of everyday misogyny. Her unofficial slogan, "shut up and play" (see Figure 2), serves as a strong reminder that it is the presence of women in gaming cultures that is considered acceptable, not their active participation or voice.[31] Palpably, Vivian James is deliberate manipulation of the media image of #gamergate to create the appearance that it includes women and accepts their inclusion in gaming cultures. But her slogan in particular has troubling connotations, which implies the desire for women to stop 'complaining' about the content of digital games and the sexist and misogynist practices of some men in gaming cultures, particularly by seeking to draw attention to the harassment they experience in those gaming cultures.

As self-perceived underdogs, some male gamers feel that criticism, critique, and attempts to otherwise reform and/or undermine the carefully constructed "us" versus "them" mentality that can still be found in gaming cultures. The restraint on Vivian James's vocal criticality suggests women should 'play' rather than use their voices to draw attention to harassment and toxic culture more generally. This functions to police the voice of women by implying the act of 'calling out' toxic behavior is an attack on the community of gamers, which exposes the underdogs to further criticism. The women who do speak out thus cannot be 'true' gamers because no true gamer would ever criticize gaming in this way. To be one of "us" means you must always be with "us", or you are against "us" and with "them". For such gamers, if women want to be included in gaming cultures they should quietly enjoy their hobby without making a fuss. However, how this silencing is enforced has other more significant and concerning implications.

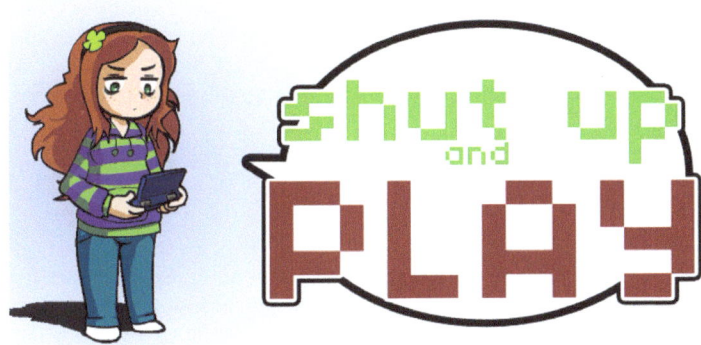

Figure 2

At the heart of Vivian James is the implied threat of sexual violence. A key design element of her iconic appearance is a deliberate embedding of a reference to the 'Daily Dose' or 'Piccolo Dick', a well-known *DragonBallZ* rape meme from 4chan's /v/ board. The green and purple stripes on her hoodie are a subcultural reference to the colors of the involved characters. This point is in no way concealed, but is part of the deliberate hostility towards women that was embodied in Vivian James by the anonymous members of the /v/ board.[32] Salter and Blodgett have pointed out that rape jokes coincide with gamer slang that is used in victory and serves to encourage a casual attitude towards sexual violence within male-dominated areas of gaming cultures.[33] This casual use of rape jokes forms a milieu where victim blaming is seen as an appropriate response to complaints about sexual harassment. The harassment coordinated against women in the games industry by #gamergate was characterized by rape threats, and other forms of suggesting the possibility of violence and exacerbating their vulnerability to violence through forms of harassment like doxxing. The threat of rape was one of the key tools in #gamergate's harassment campaigns for silencing women that they perceived as outsiders.[34] In the context of gaming cultures, male gamers may feel that they can deny culpability for the hostile environment that rape threats can create, because they are made 'in play' with an understanding that they are 'not serious.'

The power imbalance that underpins the threat of rape pushes such acts outside of the scope of play. Rape threats are "a form of violence in and of themselves." A playful rape threat, may be written off as a 'joke' by the instigator, but the recipient of the threat cannot necessarily treat it this way, as the context that frames the exchange is one of overwhelming hostility, and pointedly emphasises perceived vulnerabilty. The persistence of rape jokes and rape threats in gaming cultures thus becomes a mode for disciplining women in games who refuse to 'shut up and play.' In this logic women gamers should 'understand' that the rape threat is just a normal part of gaming culture and not act 'butthurt' about it. Thus offering a very flimsy excuse for those #gamergate supporters who might need to justify this outrageous behavior.

CONCLUSION

Vivian James showcases how #gamergate survives and flourishes through everyday expressions of misogyny. Vivian James acts as a "regulatory fiction," that polices women in gaming, particularly by commanding silence with the implied threat of rape.[36] This also suggests the general regulation of bodies in gaming through avatars, particularly what kinds of bodies are used as avatars in games. While Vivian James signals a very specific message and threat to women, avatars more generally are often criticized for the lack of inclusion of different kinds of bodies beyond the white, heterosexual male. While many games now include playable female avatars, they are often designed for the viewing pleasure of a male audience. Even fewer games include avatars who are non-white or genderqueer. These exclusions have an impact on who can see themselves as clearly included as a part of gaming culture.

If Vivian James demonstrates anything useful, it is to emphasize the importance of the avatar beyond a literal representation, as a signifier for acceptable inclusion and active agency. Just as Vivian James acts as a subtle yet powerful tool for policing participation, the availability of different avatars in a game can also signal a claim of voice and space in real-world video game culture as much as in the fictional worlds they inhabit. The organization of the funding and design for Vivian James suggests a productive way forward that will potentially allow many different kinds of bodies to be playable avatars, as gaming cultures and communities become more directly involved in the funding and design of games through crowdsourced funding. The success that #gamergate had in using crowd-funding against women, suggests that larger coalitions of diverse bodies may use the same tools to destabilize and dismantle the masculine dominance of digital games.

ACKNOWLEDGEMENTS

This chapter forms a part of the research project DP140101503 Avatars and Identities (Justin Clemens, Tom Apperley and John Frow) funded by the Australian Research Council.

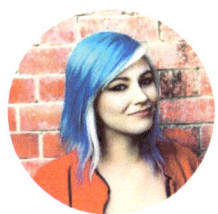

Mahli-Ann Butt is a doctoral candidate at the University of Sydney in the Departments of Media & Communication and Gender & Cultural Studies. She is the Diversity Officer for the Digital Games Research Association (DiGRA) and the Editor-in-Chief of Press Start Journal. Mahli-Ann researches the complex entanglements of online/offline and private/public spheres of gaming culture and its intersections with identity and affective labour.

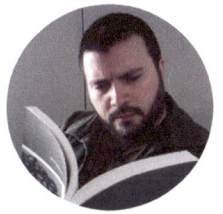

Tom Apperley is a researcher and educator specializing in digital games and other playful technologies. He is a University Researcher in the Centre of Excellence in Game Culture Studies at Tampere University, Finland.

DIGITAL CAPTURE:
PHOTOGRAMMETRY AS RHETORIC, FICTION, AND RELIC

Josh Harle, University of New South Wales

What does it mean to capture something? The term 'digital capture' has made its way into common usage to describe the act of recording an image or video via digital technology, reflecting a faith in our technologies' ability to accurately and impartially translate pieces of the world into something we can possess, carry around, archive, and share. In modern Western science, this metaphor of 'capture' has been central to practices of knowledge production; isolating and extracting knowledge from its real-world context, while obscuring the specific interpretative processes used to do this.

In this chapter I'll be exploring 'photogrammetry', a recent digital capture technology that enables the autonomous creation of 'photo-realistic' 3D representations of objects and landscapes from a set of images. Through an examination of the design decisions and representational aesthetic of photogrammetry, and its typical use in scientific research, I'll show how the practice of this technology introduces an unacknowledged transformational process, discarding some aspects of the subject while focussing on and manipulating others.

In doing so, this chapter argues that the resulting reconstructions are active cultural artefacts themselves, as forms of rhetoric, fiction, and relic of the world-view that produced them.

PHOTOGRAMMETRY

The word photogrammetry is derived from the conjunction of 'photograph' (itself 'light' and 'writing') and 'measuring'. Early photogrammetry was a labour-intensive process of identifying and triangulating reference points from multiple photographs to calculate angles and distances, producing real-world measurements.[1] Current photogrammetry software uses an approach called Structure from Motion (SfM); extending the principles of earlier photogrammetry by automating the analysis of images through the use of computer image processing.[2]

Modern photogrammetry effectively gives the user an automated way of creating a 3D model of an object or environment, without the need for prior knowledge of the subject or even the camera used to record it. By taking a set of images of a subject from different viewpoints, a user can reconstruct the geometry and texture (surface colour) information of the subject, with the process internally handling the feature-matching, camera estimation, and triangulation.

The stages of the process can be summarised as:

1. Detecting and extracting suitable 'feature points' from each photograph,
2. Comparing feature points to find those shared across several images,
3. Progressively improving an estimate of the 3D position model of features to find the best-fit of feature points and camera positions, and filtering outliers and unmatched points,
4. Projecting out from camera positions towards shared feature points, triangulating depth to produce a sparse 'point cloud' of shared features in 3D space,
5. Expanding the point cloud by triangulating individual image pixels, working outward from known feature positions, based on similar colour,
6. Creating a watertight surface (a 'mesh' in computer modelling language) that best fits the dense point cloud, (see Figure 1)
7. Projecting the original image from each camera onto this surface, averaging different colours and lighting across views.

This method of photogrammetry is particularly robust in detecting and removing 'outlier' details. Photos can be taken at different times (potentially months or years apart), and any variation in the appearance of the subject will be ignored given enough shared feature-points to form a 'consensus model'. In an early example of the potential for SfM-based photogrammetry, researchers sourced images of the *Notre Dame de Paris* pulled from community photo collections such as *Flickr* and *Panoramio* to build a 3D model of the cathedral.[3] As these

TECHNOLOGY AS CULTURAL PRACTICE

images were mostly amateur tourist photos, they often included participants posing in front of the cathedral and occluding (blocking out) part of the detail, but by ignoring any inconsistent features not shared across multiple images, photogrammetry successfully combined data from photos taken years apart to create a complete model with a comparable level of detail and accuracy to reference laser scans.[4]

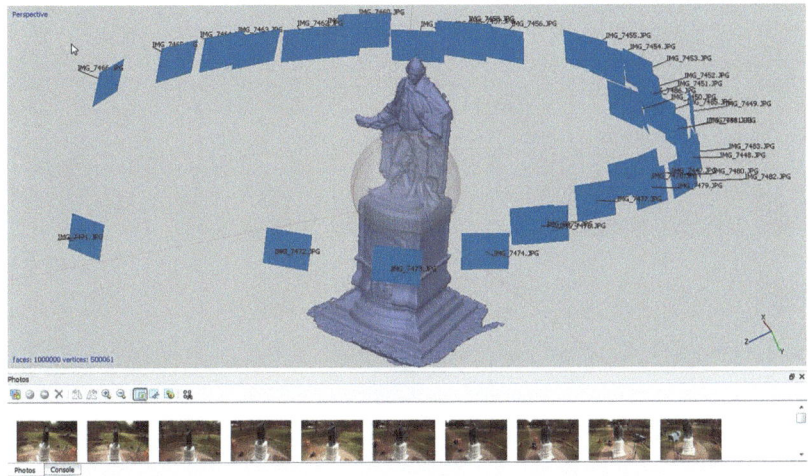

Since my introduction to and initial experimentation with photogrammetry as a digital artist and researcher, SfM has been progressively optimised and improved, with *Stages 4, 5, 6,* and *7* only practically available (i.e. as a compiled 'binary' application rather than source code) post-2010. The accessibility of available tools has grown from extremely limited (experimental code running only within a Linux environment), to broad (an ecology of commercial software for Mac, Windows, and even mobile devices) automating a process that is currently hundreds of times faster than eight years ago, thanks to improved code, increases in computer processing power, and the use of the graphics card *Graphics Processing Unit* (GPU) to process image data in an optimised way.

This process is extremely powerful, automatically producing what appears to be an incredibly accurate reconstruction that can be rendered as an animation, or exported as a standard 3D model for further modelling or 3D printing (see Figure 2). However, the process inevitably generates areas of visibly incorrect geometry. Where images provide multiple viewpoints of an object's shape, there will be a dense collection of points in the point cloud, and the resulting mesh will conform to these points to produce a detailed surface. Where there is less

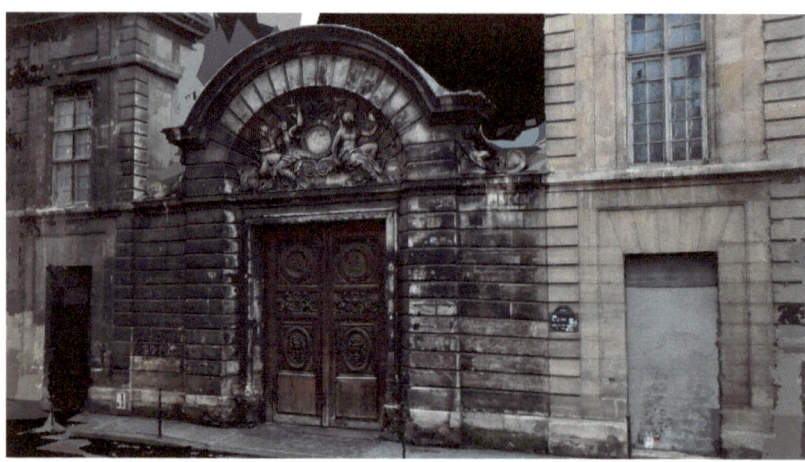

Figure 2

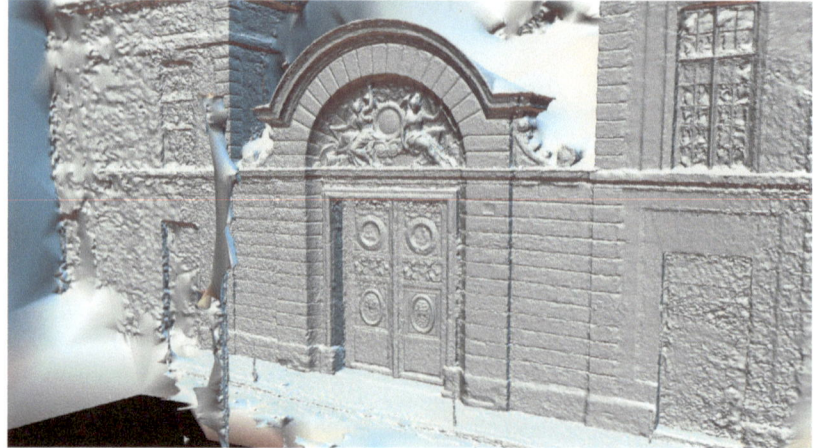

Figure 3

overlap of photographs, or where parts of an object are occluded by overhangs or obstacles, the process will fail to produce enough features points, and the reconstruction section devolves into liquiform blobs (see edges of Figure 3). Within common photogrammetry software a tool is provided to allow users to easily 'crop' the model to remove these undesired artefacts where they occur at the edges of a model. While the process simultaneously reconstructs the original camera positions, it is typical for these to be discarded rather than represented in the final outcome.

USE IN WESTERN SCIENCE

From the beginning, the development of photogrammetry, like cartography, closely conformed to the concept of 'capture' and (by association) its ties to military conquest, as a way of producing usable representations of space:

> [...]the notion that real objects or landscapes could be replaced by their photographic images was central to the whole concept of photogrammetry, [with early photogrammetry proponent Oliver Wendell Holmes stating] in 1859 that the most significant feature of photography was that it "divorced" form from matter: "In fact, matter as a visible object is of no great use any longer, except as the mould on which form is shaped." [Adding:] "Give us a few negatives of a thing worth seeing, taken from different points of view, and that is all we want of it. Pull it down or burn it up, if you please." From the very beginning, the substitution of objects with images had the potential of construction as well as destruction. Military applications of photogrammetry in the 20th century made wide use of the latter.[5]

While modern military uses of photogrammetry remain opaque, contemporary scientific applications have developed in response to the technology's particular strengths and weaknesses. Since SfM removes the necessity of human labour to identify and match feature-points across images, photogrammetry can build models based on tracking tens of thousands of unique features across thousands of images. The limitation of this process is that the subject must exhibit the type of features that can be reliably detected and tracked by the computer-vision algorithm in *Stage 1*.

In order to be effective, photogrammetry must have a subject-matter that is non-reflective (reflection would cause the object surface to appear different from different angles), no large areas of undifferentiated colour, and have a high density of 'interesting' and non-repeating features (that allow for unambiguous matching of sections between photos, and later, point triangulation). For this reason, interior spaces with large areas of uniformly-coloured walls generally produce poor results, while weathered, eroded, or graffitied buildings work very well, as do natural rock formations, rock art, and petroglyphs. Archaeologists and geologists were quick to realise that the sort of sites they work with were well-suited to photogrammetry, and adopted its use into their research, replacing photographic documentation as an analysis and communication tool, with reconstructed 3D models.[6]

The use of photogrammetry allowed archaeologists to quickly document a site: photos can be taken relatively haphazardly and without worrying about framing key features, with the emphasis on a large number of overlapping images from different angles. Returning from field-work and in the comfort of their research labs they could process the images into a 3D digital 'replica' of a site, to interrogate and analyse in their own time (enhancing colours, producing 'orthographic projections' and site maps), and providing them with a valuable tool to present compelling, 'high-tech' visualisations that showed off both their technical competency and depth of knowledge of a site. In comparison to traditional photographic documentation, which tries to visually communicate meaningful features of a site via framing, and the supplementary, time-consuming task of taking physical measurements, photogrammetry allows for significant features to be identified after the fact. With photogrammetry it's possible to focus on the task of photographing from many angles without occlusion, and, once reconstructed, to 'see' the site as a whole, think about what is 'present' in the scene, and take measurements.

Archaeological fieldwork often takes place in remote and hard-to-reach areas that can require chartered helicopter flights and sometimes hours of hiking to access the site. While archaeologists have had access to laser scanning equipment that similarly produces 3D models, photogrammetry introduced a cheap and easy way of quickly 'reconstructing' a site. In comparison to hiking with a heavy and fragile laser scanning kit, tripod, and batteries, finding appropriate locations to set it up, waiting the several minutes each scan rotation took (a site scan would typically take around 2 hours), and dealing with the inevitable problem of large gaps in reconstruction where an occluding feature 'shadowed' the laser, a researcher could hike with just a consumer digital camera, shoot images without much consideration, and complete the documentation in 20 minutes. This generally produced a more complete model than the laser scan with a comparable level of detail, making 3D capture a practical and accessible tool for archaeologists.[7]

THE CULTURE OF DIGITAL CAPTURE

The philosopher Bruno Latour was prominent in developing a critical examination of the culture at work in Western science, taking the novel move of engaging in 'embedded field-work' within laboratories to watch what scientists actually did. He observed a pointed contrast between the public face of Western science as a linear, rational, acultural process, and the ad-hoc practices and social negotiations required of scientists in their research. His analysis has been instrumental in the opening up of Western science to discussions around cultural practices.[8]

In previous research,[9] I have investigated emerging spatial technologies (e.g. Augmented Reality, geo-tagged social platforms), their adherence to a tech culture of mapping and data capture, and how, given the underlying systems and aesthetics of these technologies, they could be re-appropriated to generate new meanings. I suggested that while these technologies appeared to present "a level of uninhibited peer-to-peer communication that challenges monolithic structures of knowledge and suggests a meaning-giving system based on democratic participation", in normal use these systems are restricted to "representing propositional statements of space using methods developed as part of geometric and productive logic".[10]

There is a rich field of critical analysis around analogue image capture technologies, with theorists such as David Thomas exploring the influence Western scientific culture had on the development of visual technologies, i.e. the "historical or cultural frame of reference [informing the technologies'] modes of production and reproduction, and the interrelationships between their specialized cultures and those of other technologies". [11]

As an extension of such work, this chapter investigates an emerging technology that has not yet developed to the point of significant everyday social impact. In describing both the mechanics and practice of photogrammetry in detail, from the perspective of someone involved (peripherally) in its early development and use, my intent is to give theorists and artists a head-start: opening up this powerful, emerging technology to critical interrogation, and siting it in the context of the dominant drives and world-view of Western science.

In addition to suggesting the ways in which photogrammetry has been *shaped* by this culture, this chapter identifies three 'lenses' for viewing the practice of photogrammetry by scientists (and the resulting reconstruction) as *an active part* of the reproduction of this culture, as the operation of **rhetoric**, the composing of **fictions**, and the generation of science **relics**, discussed below.

RHETORIC

In the use of photogrammetry for scientific research, the reconstruction forms part of scientists' attempt to stake a claim to authority. Not only must the individual reconstruction be convincingly 'true to nature' (the abstracted product appearing equivalent to the original), it must also do its part to convince its audience that the abstractive process itself is legitimate.

In *Science in action: How to follow scientists and engineers through society,* Latour describes how fundamental the social process of convincing others is to the practice of science. Where the mythology of the Scientific Method states that 'once the scientists have the right answer it will convince everyone', the actual process of establishing accepted ideas is one of winning over detractors: "Once the machine works people will be convinced" vs "the machine will work when all the relevant people are convinced".[12] In one anecdote he describes Jim Watson and Francis Crick (the discoverers of the double-helix structure of DNA) waiting for metal models of chemical bases to arrive before they could present their theory — their model had to be robust to be convincing, and their flimsy cardboard bases would have not been persuasive.[13]

How do we begin to understand the mechanisms by which a digital representation can be convincing? In *The rhetoric of persuasive games*, game theorist Anders Løvlie goes back to Aristotle's description of 'rhetoric', as a model for understanding forms of communication intending to persuade.[14] According to this, rhetorical speech has three means of persuasion: moral character (*ethos*), reasoning (*logos*), and emotional affect (*pathos*), with Aristotle suggesting *ethos* as the strongest of the three. Notably, *ethos* and *pathos* are part of the practical performance of the speech, and have nothing to do with the argument being made; the power to convince lies in the speaker stating the claim in a way 'worthy of credence'.

The most basic tool photogrammetry uses to convince the audience is perhaps the most seemingly innocuous and straightforward: it is a *visual* representation. Vision holds a special place in the Western conception of knowledge and truth[15]; what architectural theorist Juhani Pallasmaa identifies as "the ocular-centric tradition and the consequent spectator theory of knowledge in Western thinking".[16] By choosing to represent only the visual elements of a site to stand in for the whole, photogrammetry demonstrates the privileged position vision holds in the communication of knowledge.

Ahmed El Antably, an early researcher in the use of (manually modelled) 3D virtual environments in archaeology, has argued that the symbolic realism of the virtual environment is persuasive in itself, presenting historically ambiguous knowledge in a (virtual) robust, concrete form (objects and structures realised in a particular arrangement, and navigable as a 3D space), leading to both the "suspension of disbelief" and the "suspension of imagination". He insists this must be acknowledged and responded to by the archaeologists using speculative 3D reconstruction.[17]

Early forms of photogrammetry leveraged the perceived reliability of photography for capturing a subject, co-opting the mathematical properties of projection into an argument for the legitimacy of process in general:

> *Bound by linear perspective, photography turned huge mountain landscapes and rock formations into flat and manageable images that were "optically consistent." Bruno Latour, borrowing the term from William Ivins, has stressed the importance of this quality of images for scientific work: "In linear perspective, no matter from what distance and angle an object is seen, it is always possible to transfer it—to translate it—and to obtain the same object at a different size as seen from another position."[18]*

In contrast, modern photogrammetry reconstructions don't articulate an argument for the process at all – the logic (*logos*) of the underlying automated process is hidden to the viewer as well as the creator. Instead, credibility (*ethos*) is communicated via the techno-scientific aesthetic of the result (e.g. the visual/representational language of computer-generated images), and *pathos* by the 'sense' of accuracy in the reconstruction (e.g. the emotional affect generated by the image of the Paris door reconstruction).

It's important to note that since photogrammetry is very rarely done with reference to other forms of measurement, the 'success' of the reconstruction isn't judged on comparitive accuracy. As with Latour's criteria for a working scientific machine, the photogrammetric reconstruction will 'work' when the results look convincing to the practitioner, and it is usual for the process to be repeated through trial-and-error reconfiguration of settings only until a convincing-looking reconstruction is produced.

In applying the concept of rhetoric to digital media, Løvlie mobilises Roland Barthes' writing *Rhetoric of the Image*, describing how a collection of specific images (signifiers) in an advertisement are used to form a persuasive argument. Similarly, photogrammetry's ability to convince is aided by utilising signifiers of scientific accuracy, objectivity, and authority (the computer simulation, 3D render), and cropping out signifiers of inaccuracy or error (such as the distorted outlier edges of models).

Objectivity and the 'God's-eye view'

Western science presents its knowledge in a way that attempts to claim objectivity and universality. As a consequence, indications of the (literal and conceptual) perspectives of individual researchers are removed, or at least neutralised (i.e. through standard conventions of photography, lab work), and replaced by an abstract 'objective' perspective. As David Turnbull argues in *Masons, tricksters and cartographers: Comparative studies in the sociology of scientific and indigenous knowledge*:

> It is this claim to be able to produce mimetic totalising theory that Western culture has used simultaneously to promote and reinforce its own stability and dominance[...] It constitutes part of the ideological justification of scientific objectivity, the 'god-trick' [...]: the illusion that there can be a positionless vision of everything.[19]

In virtual representations, perspective is deeply important to communicate the relationship of the observer to the fictional world. In 'first person' computer games, the player's perspective is tied to a virtual body 'on the ground', moving around the environment as one would walking: "the [point of view] is associated with the user's position and with 'me' – it represents subjectivity within the computer-generated scene."[20] The player is given an identity and a role in a story, with particular interests and desires that play out in the game. In contrast, 'strategy' games give the player a 'god's-eye-view' of the environment, generally free to exercise their whim as a city planner, general, or even literal god.

In photogrammetry, as with Computer-Aided Design (CAD) programs and strategy games, the observer is untethered from the seeing the landscape as pedestrian (or photographer, crouching and craning to achieve shots). The user has complete control to move around the scene unimpeded, or alternatively to move the reconstruction around, shift its scale, crop or manipulate it:

> [...giving] the impression that the entire object of manipulation is moving while the camera stays still – like you're rotating a small toy in your hands.[21]

The user is also given the power to shift the perspective into an abstract 'orthographic projection', a linear representation that removes the perception of distance from the model (no foreshortening as parts of the model become distant to the viewer, as they would in the world). The ability to snap the model to various section-views transforms the spatial representation of the model into one of abstracted knowledge, represented in an imaginary, purportedly "knowledge-centered",[22] linear spatial system of Euclidean geometry. This is a way of seeing that no human eye can achieve, an image "in which the viewpoint is set at an infinite distance, effectively a 'view from nowhere.'"[23]

TECHNOLOGY AS CULTURAL PRACTICE

'Realism' and the appearance of authenticity

The appearance of authenticity (know as '*verisimilitude*') is more important than truth (correspondence with reality) in making a convincing argument. For photogrammetry, with tools such as the provocatively-named *Capturing Reality*, this sense of authenticity rests in its 'photo-realism', described by media theorist Lev Manovich as "the ability to simulate any object in such a way that its computer image is indistinguishable from its photograph".[24]

Manovich argues that our ability to accept 'photo-realistic' computer-generated images as real rests on the persuasive power of more than a hundred and fifty years of film and photography,[25] with early practitioners convinced of its 'epistemological supremacy' over the eye (its ability to capture truth) by its ability to capture parts of a scene we wouldn't notice in person.[26] Similarly, in the progressive development of virtual environments for computer games, a sense of authenticity is created by including in the level design elements that typically wouldn't be considered important or worthy of reproduction in non-narrative representations or earlier games (rubbish, graffiti, toilets, etc.).[27]

Modern photogrammetry does a very good job of representing small, easily missed details, resulting in a strong sense of verisimilitude. The particular mechanics of the SfM process means that feature points are detected most successfully from aspects of the original scene that seem insignificant to a human observer (and only included in the most painstakingly thorough sketch or model). Dents and marks on a surface provide a dense collection of points to form a mesh, resulting in these minor physical features being even more detailed than the surrounding model.

To convince their audience, archaeologists must present their reconstruction with the right indicators of objectivity, and appearance of authenticity, using a representational style that encourages the suspension of disbelief. For the most part, these signifiers and aesthetics are provided for them by the photogrammetry software, but their implicit rhetorical sensibilities are exercised in the convention of cropping out models at the boundaries of convincing geometry.

So far, photogrammetry seems to be sufficiently persuasive. By Latour's description, a convincing claim or scientific instrument will remain a 'black box', the contents and mechanisms at work inside left hidden and unquestioned: "If there is no controversy [...] then it is useless to go on talking about interpretations, representation, a biased or distorted world-view, weak or fragile pictures of the world".[28] However, the signifiers needed for persuasion are effectively cultural, and what constitutes a 'realistic' digital model are related to viewer literacy and developments in technology (as we see in the development of computer games). These have changed over time, and will continue to change.

FICTION

Regardless of how convincing a photogrammetric reconstruction is, the results are always the outcome of a creative interpretation: photogrammetry software is designed to produce a coherent object, and where there's not enough data, it will fake it. The surface is a consensus model between different photographs, light and shadows 'baked' onto the surface as a composition produced from mixing all photographs. Variations in the estimation of the camera properties will produce distortion in the geometry, and the nature of the underlying process (an approximated best-fit calculated using the fast-but-imprecise GPU) means even two results from identical datasets will produce slightly different results. The process is even likely to produce geometry that never existed, chiastic models stitching together two parts of a subject from different times, where a later, altered (eroded, repaired, vandalised) surface from one part is combined with the older view of another section.

The final reprojection stage in photogrammetry does something akin to theatre 'flats' or backdrops: without the colour applied, we have a white surface that reveals the shape and detail of the object mesh, and inaccuracies and potentially low-resolution areas are easy to spot. However, once the original view of the camera is 'painted' over the surface, the accuracy of the geometry (the shape of the model) is obscured. There may be distortion of this surface due to reconstruction errors, but when viewed from an angle close to that of the original set of cameras, regardless of the accuracy of the geometry, the object will look identical, i.e. a convincing facade.

Through the software's focus on automation and visually 'consistent' results, the reconstruction decisions, errors, mistakes, and best-guesses are hidden to the viewer as well as the creator, and the process feels like a neutral, objective, and accurate process. Unless the user of the technology has technical knowledge of the mechanics of photogrammetry, they are unlikely to be aware of the artificiality of the process, and take the solidity of the reconstruction 'at face value'.

To the layperson, the contingency and performative aspects of science are hidden, and the results seem like a solid and consistent whole with no indication of the messy specifics of its creation. In substituting traditional photography for photogrammetry, researchers are able to conceal more of the process of forming research, no longer having to acknowledge the obvious: that the process of producing the knowledge was a performative one, that a particular photo had to be taken *by someone*.

In a photo of an object, there is no 'true object' represented: the image formed is a result of the specific conditions under which the photo was taken. Any captured element of the surface of the object is subject to the time of day, lighting source, shadows, atmospherics, depth of field and focus, its level of exposure, colour grading and image quality, people present in the scene, where the photographer was standing, and even the height of the photographer.

In contrast, the 3D models produced by photogrammetry operate with a different epistemological modality (making a different type of knowledge claim): 3D models are representations that blur out and modify specific details in the formation of a consensus of data points, but seem like robust, 'real' objects.

However, the site as represented via photogrammetry has never existed: never visited when it is neither day nor night, when there has been no sound, never been seen from a disembodied perspective, never existed as an immaterial surface of colour and nothing else, never been hacked out of its context in the landscape to float in the ether, never been an object without meaningful scale that can be rotated and resized at a whim. The isolated object is a fictional interpretation, an attempt to crop the boundaries of its existence at exactly the point the extra detail becomes unimportant for the academic field's practice of analysis.

Once introduced to the intricacies of the photogrammetry process, it might seem that the researchers responsible for developing it as a tool of digital capture are deliberately misleading us. To a critical philosopher, it was hard to imagine that the mythology behind Western science's claim of equivalence wasn't obvious to the experts who perpetuate it: "[Conceptual engineers] cannot [fail to] perceive the fictive character instilled in an order by its relationship to everyday reality. [...]But they must *not* acknowledge this relationship."[29] But it is exactly because this fiction is a manifestation of culture (an implicit world-view, ideas, customs, and social behaviour) that it is invisible to those who inhabit it. As a young computer scientist, I too was comforted by the prospect of 'making sense' of the world through digital technology, and by the circular logic of Western science, anything that cannot be empirically grasped — 'proved' and recorded — is illusionary, and thus does not need to be captured.

RELIC

In a previous paper,[30] I've described the historical transformation of maps that progressively erased signs of the performance and contingency of their creation-process from view. From their medieval form as an itinerary of stops on a pilgramage (with distances indicated in walking time), through a graphic representation featuring illustrations of the ships and survey parties involved in the creation of the map, to contemporary maps, there has been a removal of any indication of the activities and practices needed for their creation.

In commenting on the map's transformation of practices into reductive objects, spatial theorist Michel de Certeau emphasises what has been lost in the final product:

> However useful this "flattening out" may be, it transforms the temporal articulation of places into a spatial sequence of points. A graph takes the place of an operation...[It is] a mark in place of acts, *a relic in place of performances*: it is only their remainder, the sign of their erasure. Such a projection postulates that it is possible to take the one (the mark) for the other (operations articulated on occasions).[31]

Similarly, as a form of digital capture used by scientists, photogrammetry cuts out all but a visible trace of a site (e.g. ambient sound-scape, materiality of the surface, people present in the shots, the wider context of the site in the landscape), and hides any sign of the actions of the researcher or the process itself.

This absence isn't due to technical limitations; it's a decision made in the development of photogrammetry software, and by scientific practitioners. Years before the Washington University Computer Vision Lab developed the tools for reconstructing detailed geometry, they produced *PhotoSynth*, a 'photo tourism' tool (see Figure 4). This allowed photographs to be navigated in a 3D space according to their detected camera positions, with the viewer travelling through a spatial field of photographs, transitioning smoothly between each to show the journey from one viewpoint to another.[32]

Only one software package (*Capturing Reality*) currently makes use of the camera position data normally discarded from photogrammetry, to create animated visuals (of the complete, consistent model). This could be extended to create reconstructions from video that narrate the practices of documentation while illustrating the image-by-image process of reconstructing a 3D model. Such an approach would emphasise the performative act of composing a reconstruction, while showing the underlying logic at work in the algorithm (effectively illustrating its imprecise, consensus-building nature), as a recognisable shape is slowly refined out of an inchoate blob.

It seems poetically appropriate to identify photogrammetry reconstructions as 'relics' of Western science and digital capture culture: in trying to grasp pieces of other cultures, the practice of scientists produces a shell; a sign of the erasure. As suggested above, the persuasiveness of these digital relics does not age well as our digital literacy improves. It seems likely that current reconstructions will be of interest primarily for illustrating current Western scientific practices, and that like 19th-century photogrammetry images, they will have only 'historic value' as a representation of "a very particular, individual stage of development of a certain productive realm of mankind."[33]

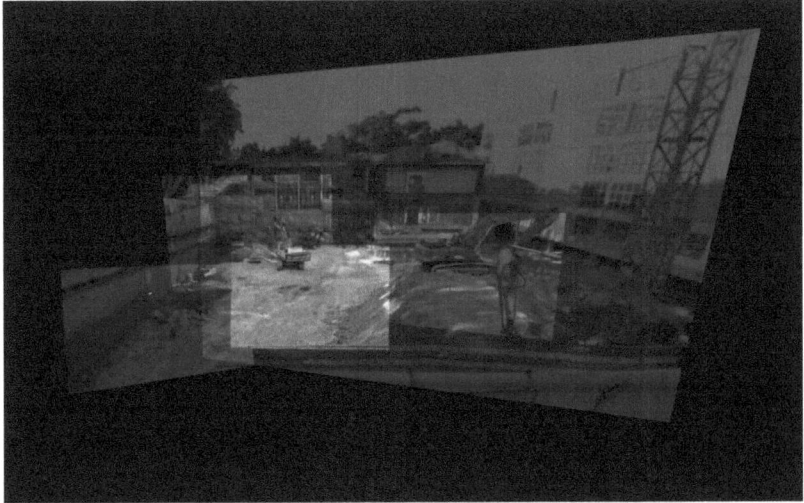

Figure 4

EVADING CAPTURE; DIGITAL SPATIAL STORYTELLING

Is it possible to use photogrammetry in a way that does not conform to the culture of Western science? Yes, of course. Photogrammetry is designed with certain uses in mind, which influence the design decisions built into it, but the technology is not deterministic. My own media art practice focuses on tactics for re-appropriating established and emerging capture technologies (e.g. laser scanning, photogrammetry, drone image-capture) as expressive mediums, altering their practice and outcomes to introduce an affective element normally absent. The resulting works embrace rather than hide their performative origins, and reflect the contingency of the creative process.

In response to a similar critical interrogation of the history and politics at work in mapping, the creative practice of 'radical cartography' has expanded the expressive potential of maps while addressing the power inequalities it has traditionally reproduced,[34] and emerging creative uses of photogrammetry show the diversity of practices around 3D digital capture technology (e.g. *Palimpsest* — figure 5).

We can look to creative practices such as digital media art for examples of very different cultures of photogrammetry, where identifying and acknowledging the performative nature of photogrammetry, and the gaps and artefacts it produces, gives practitioners the opportunity to explore its limits, allowances, and expressive potential. Such uses can subvert 'scientific' knowledge-producing technologies to help us tell stories that 'make sense' of a world of digitally mediated experience.

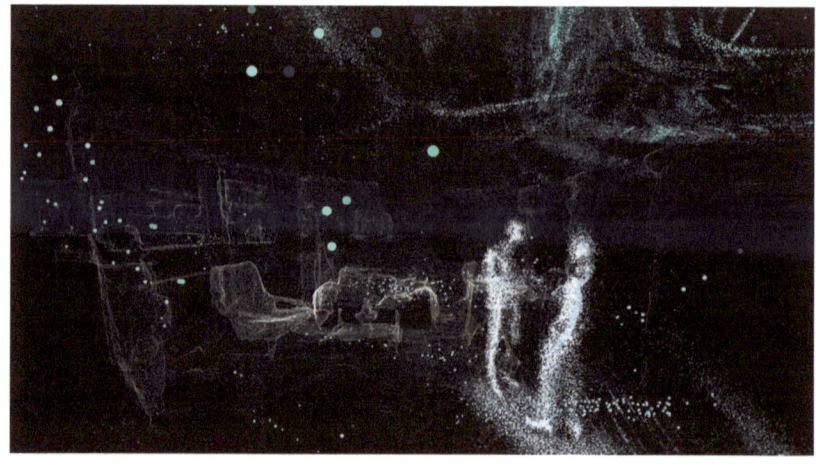

Figure 6

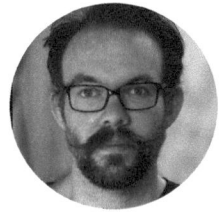

Dr Josh Harle is a multidisciplinary researcher and media artist with a background in computer science and cybernetics, philosophy, and fine arts. His practice explores the contemporary use of digital technologies to map and make sense of the world. He is the founder and director of Tactical Space Lab, an experimental VR studio, and a UNSW Art & Design Visiting Fellow.

BEYOND IMPERIAL TOOLS: FUTURE-PROOFING TECHNOLOGY THROUGH INDIGENOUS GOVERNANCE AND TRADITIONAL KNOWLEDGE SYSTEMS

Angie Abdilla, Old Ways, New

Australian Aboriginal peoples are the oldest living continuous culture, from the driest continent on Earth. Ancient technology developed by Aboriginal peoples reveals underlying design and development methodologies that reflect a unified approach and value system. Aboriginal social cohesion, well-being, environmental sustainability, culture and spirituality underpins the foundation of such innovation and has been nurtured through systems of governance, commonly understood as Lore.[1] It is these relational, cultural practices which have created the framework for this society and the myriad science and technology developments produced by Aboriginal peoples over millennia. Given contemporary global challenges, it is a critical time to reflect on what we can learn from such frameworks, and to initiate a new wave of technologies designed and developed through a Code of Ethics, embodying the principles of social and environmental sustainability: *Caring for Country, Caring for Kin*. By adopting Australian Aboriginal Lore, ethical technology would help to bring about the changes required to address fractured political, economic and social systems. In the following paper, I discuss how the development of a new Code of Ethics for technology development can be informed by Aboriginal design principles and governance.

The seeds for writing this chapter were planted four years ago through a curiosity to understand the different trajectories of Aboriginal and Western technologies, and what is required to create culturally relevant and grounded technologies for Aboriginal peoples into the future. During this short time, emerging technologies have continued to extend the influence of an anthropocentric economic understanding of the world, resulting in the acceleration of technologies' drive to synthesis and commoditise what makes us human: *consciousness*.

The raft of technology ethics frameworks, mainly developed by the private sector but increasingly also nation states, have typically focused on the prevention of artificial intelligence (AI) being developed in ways that may harm human (the individual), economic, and political systems. These frameworks are reactive attempts to respond to the negative impacts of technology which have manifested many times before in recent history, and tend to be limited by the speculative/imaginative ability of those who create them. Meanwhile, ongoing work with Elders and industry practitioners has revealed the values, principles and practices behind Aboriginal technologies designed around social and environmental sustainability. Through this understanding, it is clear Indigenous governance provides an existing, time-proven ethical framework for the development of new technologies. Central to this framework is the development of individual technologies within the context of a wider system of governance, which ensures that broader consequences are not ignored and new developments are not compartmentalised. As Jason Lewis states, *"we do it because we believe that Indigenous epistemologies are much better at respectfully accommodating the non-human[...] ultimately, our goal is that we, as a species figure out how to treat these new non-human kin respectfully and reciprocally - and not as mere tools, or worse, slaves to their creators[2]."*

This chapter reviews Aboriginal peoples' governance systems through the reciprocal relationship with land that has informed the development of these innately spirited and conscious technologies based upon inherent principles of sustainability for both humans and the environment. I will detail the origins of these technologies, and the *ensoulment or psychology-of-place[3]* which inhabit Indigenous Techno-Animism. By reviewing the origins of Aboriginal relational interconnection and interrelatedness with Country, and the agency of Western technology and its influences from the Eurocentric, 'man harnessing nature' Enlightenment-era thinking, will reveal the dissociation of humanity and the earth of the Western model. Through doing so, we will contrast how Western cultural and social structures have created the foundations for contemporary technology development and illustrate how Aboriginal design principles embedded in these technologies can assist in the futuring of *Deep Technologies[4]* for the ethical and considered advancement of humankind and our environment.

INDIGENOUS LORE: GOVERNANCE AND ETHICS

Aboriginal Australia is a continent of 500 Nations with discreet languages, territories, customs and laws which are underpinned by Lore (otherwise known as The Dreaming or Jukkapurra). Lore embodies all culture, kinship systems and Country itself. Within these systems, relationships and experiences are encoded in a unified set of values and principles. As a complex society, Aboriginal creation stories typically share a similar focus on how different creator beings brought the earth, the land and waterways, animals and humankind into being. Where Christian creation has Man as transcendent and pinnacle, in the image of God, Aboriginal creation stories position humankind as a derivative part of Country itself. The fundamental basis of Lore is therefore *a law of nature*, with humankind fitting into rather on top of the land itself.

Aboriginal societies developed through a custodial ethic: the repetition of an action such as that, gradually over time, the ethic becomes the norm[5]. These rights, rituals and customs are firmly rooted by a deep, symbiotic relationship to Country itself and are the basis of Aboriginal cultural practices. To fully comprehend this relationship we need to understand Country as an entity, both materially and non-materially. Country encompasses the sky, sun and moon; the seas and waterways; mountains and land; fauna and flora, the earth and everything held within it; the stars and space itself. It's both the subterranean and metaphysics of land and is the one and only single source of Truth. For Aboriginal peoples, Country is the 'Law of Reciprocity'. There are three main distinctions which help to distinguish Lore from Western concepts of Law:

1. Aboriginal Lore is a religion,
2. a science (it can be likened to a cognitive science or applied psychology),
3. and an action guide to living and understanding reality[6].

INDIGENOUS KNOWLEDGE SYSTEMS: PATTERN THINKING AND PATTERN RECOGNITION

Within the context of Lore, I have previously identified 'Pattern Thinking' as "a system for understanding the complex web of ontology, epistemology and interrelatedness within the Indigenous paradigm"[7]. Furthermore, Pattern Recognition[8] is the deep consciousness that comes from this uninterrupted way of seeing, being and knowing. This is the non-colonial state, and our uninterrupted *old ways*:

IKS [Indigenous Knowledge Systems] can nudge the existential compartmentalism of Western techno-science into another realm of interrelationship and interconnectedness; indeed, the current wave of "new materialisms" bears striking resemblance to, and could benefit from, indyamarra[9] [a sense of the sacred; to give honour to; show respect; and to do slowly].

Mukgrrngal[10] tells me that 'the rock over there does not exist until its sung into being' and adds that the power of matter interrelationship is such that 'if we stop caring for Country, Country dies, and we die'.

In Pattern Thinking, the rock has value, meaning and place, as do human beings and the animal, plant, cosmological and metaphysical worlds combined. All things create the complexity of the Pattern Thinking web in a nuanced relationship of being and knowing entwined.

Where once religion informed and influenced all aspects of Western society, now technologist corporations are increasingly informing and influencing our worldviews [...] Pattern Thinking can regulate the delicate balance of all things synthetic and our relationship to them. It is an ethical intelligence and embodiment born from this land, giving meaning and relationship to everything. I take this system, evolved as a streamlined ecology, as the best chance of Australian humanity's maximising its chances of success.[11]

Aboriginal peoples use a strict code to bind the veracity of oral language for the custodianship of often critical and complex information and the regulation of its transmission throughout successive generations, over hundreds of thousands of years. The vast reservoir of knowledge including fauna and flora, astronomy and space itself required to ensure the health and wellbeing of both Kin and Country meant that Aboriginal people needed to have encyclopaedic memories. So how do those old people recall such vast volumes of knowledge? Through the physical practicing of culture, its rituals, protocols and customs, with repetition the encoded knowledges are revealed.

Information bound within the code includes the mapping of locations, such as vital sources of water, food and shelter; complex kinship laws to protect the biophysical diversity for the health and interrelationships of clans; how to manage biodiversity of flora and fauna resources for environmental sustainability; trade relationships and the management of sovereign territories for peace-keeping; and the guidance of spiritual and cultural practices for the collective wellbeing and advancement of Country and Kin. Strict protocols exist to ensure the custodian- and stewardship of Country and the veracity and pertinence of its knowledges are kept intact through the lived, embodiment of the knowledge system. The custodianship and sharing of any story in Aboriginal culture is regarded as of critical importance; to tell the story the 'proper way' or risk contaminating knowledges and impacting potentially fatal consequences.

For example, a Songline or story to navigate vast territories and distances needs to be sung, danced and/or told with the correct intonation, pace, tone, repetition and narrative to ensure current and future generations have the correct information to destinations, such as sacred sites and vital resources embedded within Country for survival in the diverse and extreme Australian landscape. Through a succession of rites and rituals as part of initiations throughout one's life, general, deep and sacred knowledges are imparted. Custodianship of such knowledges is actively practiced through ceremony to embody the spirit and vitality of this Lore and is an acknowledgment of your growing responsibility to Country and your kin.

ABORIGINAL TECHNOLOGIES

Through a millennia-old culture, the ontologies of systems, artifacts and technologies both inanimate and animate, spiritual and manmade, have come into being through their own creation stories. These technologies are founded by a deep relational belonging to place and they are intrinsically entwined within cultural identity and practices designed to *nurture* Country. A stark contrast can be drawn here with the evolution of Western technologies and perceptions of the environment as a product associated with the transformative power and drive for human enhancement.

Following is a conceptual review of Aboriginal technologies. There are no historical records extrapolating their engineering, instead, complex interrelated information is encoded within their stories. Created over a millenia, these stories defy mere mortal inception, attesting their provenance from Country and their creation by primordial animals, and or spirit beings. As Alison Page, an Aboriginal designer from the Yuin Nation reflects:

> It's the weaving of spirit, Lore, ceremony and story that imbue Indigenous systems, artifacts and technologies [...] the story embedded within the intricate decorative design of a carved shield is layered with highly nuanced meaning and knowledges that is both didactic and spiritual.[12]

Some Aboriginal technologies are so perfectly in sync within Country that to the untrained eye, they are invisible. The transformative power gained through technology - generated by and through Country - is a cultural and spiritual feedback loop for Aboriginal peoples. This is the sophistication of a Lore of reciprocity, it is the Lore of the land.

Following are three stories of Aboriginal technologies and examples of how they can inform new emerging technology design, developments and applications.

The Boomerang: A Returning Stick by Asymmetrical Lift

An Australian cultural icon, the boomerang's design ingenuity and innovation originates from the curvature of this wooden device, typically made from either mulga or wattleseed timber (see Figure 1). There are two types of boomerangs, returnable and non-returning sticks. The former are used for the herding of birds into a net, and the latter is designed to hit the target animal, such as a kangaroo or wallaby with significant force to strike or kill. Both are designed to perform one of the most complicated acts in aerodynamics: asymmetrical lift. Informed by this design, Aboriginal engineer and inventor, David Unaipon stated in 1914, twelve years before the development of the first helicopter:

> An aeroplane can be manufactured that will rise straight into the air from the ground by application of the boomerang principle. The boomerang is shaped to rise in the air according to the velocity with which it is propelled, and so can an aeroplane.[13]

The boomerang is also used as a multi-purpose hand tool and musical instrument when clapped together with another boomerang. The boomerang developed in various formations over most of Australia.

On Mornington Island, the boomerang's existence is born from the creation story of *Thuwathu*, the Rainbow Serpent:

> *Thuwathu came as a human from the south-west via the Georgina and Nicholsen Rivers making waterholes containing mermaids and water lilies. He was a high-degree law man with many power songs to provide him with strength. His origins are vaguely associated with the snake dreaming. After building a large wet weather shelter for his sacred objects, Thuwathu's sister Pulthuku has a young baby daughter, Kintitpu, Willy Wagtail, who was getting wet since she had no shelter. Pulthuku asked Thuwathu if she could put her child in his 'humpy', but he was tired and sleeping and did not answer. She made a fire to warm her. She observed a number of spaces inside Thuwathu's shelter, but each time Thuwathu replied to her successive requests by saying that a particular space was for his big knee or for his elbows, his ears, spine, feet etc. Eventually the baby died of exposure and Pulthuku mourned and cut herself. She made a bark torch and set fire to Thuwathu's shelter all around it. He was trapped inside and badly burnt. When he rolled out in pain, he cursed his sister. Thuwathu crawled away singing whilst undergoing a biological metamorphosis. He was transforming from human form into that of a serpent. As he moved, writhing in pain, he physically altered the landscape. He dug up the ground in the vicinity of his camp that by now was all on fire. The area became submerged and was extinguished by the sea. He travelled inland leaving a deep groove in his wake which is today the Dugong River.*

His back-and-forth movements made all its tributaries. Deep water holes were left at the many places where he rested. In other places, his rib bones broke off, going into the ground to become kurparra trees (Acacia alleniana). Thuwathu's blood turned into red ochre on the surrounding tidal flats, and he vomited up many animals [...] 'every place Rainbow Serpent (Serpent) travels he leaves a young Rainbow (Serpent),... he leaves his seed'.

Thuwathu's bones grew into kurparra trees, and energies are said to be still inside these trees. This tree is a most important raw material to the Lardil, used for boomerangs, spear prongs, fighting and digging sticks, etc. [...] when obtaining kurparra for making boomerangs, one must weep next to the tree and be sad at hurting it, as well as singing special songs. Boomerangs are 'sung' into be[ing] powerful for fighting and hunting, and also take on an important role in the male tjarata ceremony (obtaining the love of a woman). These special songs aim to harness the energies inside the boomerang to aid the owner [...] 'they say that the old spirit, the spirit of the tree he always come and see whether you are doing the right thing or not, according to our law'.[14]

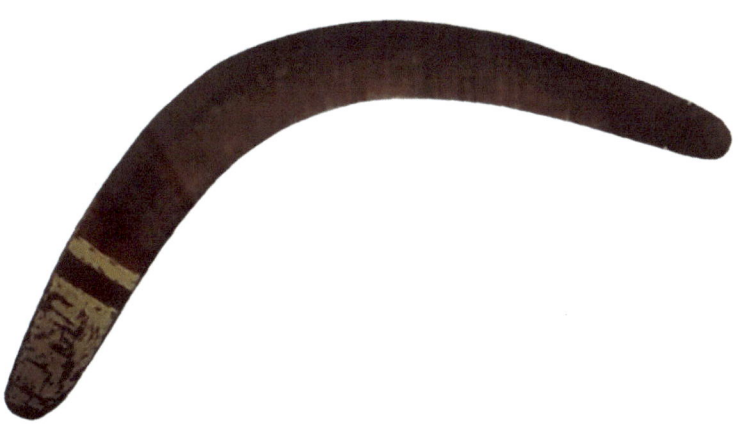

Figure 1

The Fish Trap: The World's Oldest and Largest Human-made Structure

The fish traps of Brewarrina, known as the Ngunnhu[15] by the local tribe and custodians, the Ngemba people, are the oldest human-made structure in the world, dating more than 40,000 years. Created by Baiame, a creator spirit who threw his fishing net across the Barwon, to give the shape and design of the fish traps, which his two sons, Booma-ooma-nowi and Ghinda-inda-mui then built the dry stone weirs and ponds. Biame then gave each of the traps to different family groups for their maintenance and use.[16]

As the oldest and largest structure of human origin, the fish traps are a remarkable example of dry wall construction, water ecology, animal migration and geography, engineering, hydrology and fish ecology. They are sophisticated in their simplicity of design, adaptive and responsiveness to the fluctuating highs and lows of the seasons and the river. The fish traps are made up of twelve tear-drop shaped pools spanning half a kilometre, varying in height, and a collection of stone walled weirs designed to manage the flow of fish herded into the opening of each pool before close-off (see Figure 2). Designed to ensure the flow of the river was never disrupted, whilst also resisting damage from high water flow.

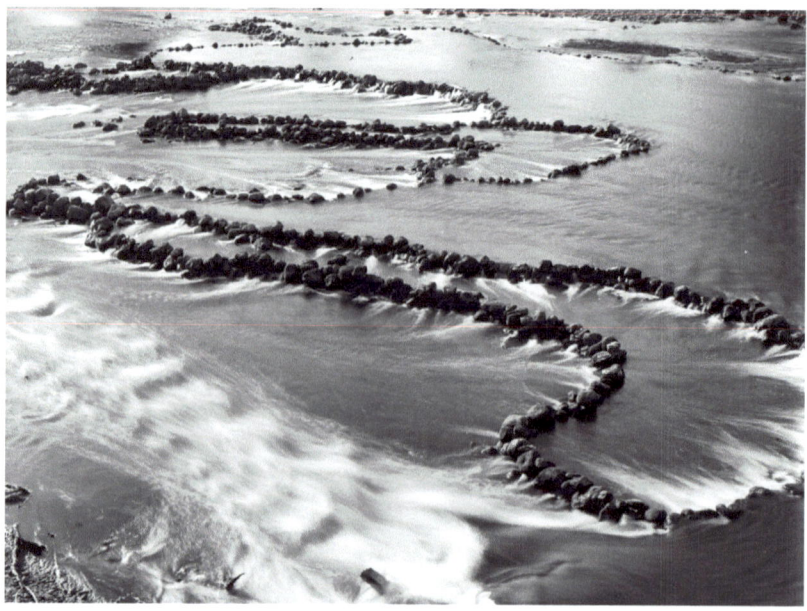

Figure 2

Archaeologists have stated that the Aboriginal peoples who designed, built and created the technology behind them must have possessed advanced knowledge of differing fields of environmental sciences. However, defying Western concepts of knowledge and provenance, the utilisation of the fish traps was guided and inspired by the pelican and the hunting techniques of this Australian bird. As Ghillar/ Michael Anderson recalls:

> There was a long drought and the people were suffering from famine. But they were saved by the pelican, which showed them how traps work by using its large beak to scoop fish out of the river. After that, the pelican became a sacred creature. If anyone hurt or killed one, that'd be the end of them. They'd be dead before they got a chance to eat it.[17]

The fish traps were also a significant meeting place for approximately twenty neighbouring tribes including the Morowari, Paarkinji, Weilwan, Barabinja, Ualarai and Kamilaroi peoples and their international[18] governing of affairs, trade, corroborees, initiations and ceremonies.[19]

Spinifex Resin: The World's First Thermoplastics

A sticky resin extracted from the plant spinifex is the world's first thermoplastic resin. Aboriginal people have been using spinifex resin for millennia for a multitude of purposes, including mounting stone heads onto spears and woomeras, repairing tools, stone walling, smoke signals and house construction. Spinifex grows across 20% of mainland Australia in dry and nutrient poor soils and hot climates (see Figure 3). The resin is extracted through a process of threshing, beating the harvested spinifex till the resin drips from the dry, tough fibres. Traditionally, the droplets are then collected and applied to heat, sometimes in the form of a burning hot rock to heat and mould the resin into a malleable mass. Aboriginal people from nations spanning the mainland of Australia have utilised spinifex resins in the production of the woomera - a spear thrower which has four times the kinetic energy of an arrow from a compound bow. The resin sets like concrete and acts as a binder for making paint from ochre.

Spinifex has recently been developed by non-Indigenous scientists in partnership with the Indjalandji-Dhidhanu people, to extract nanocellulose for a super strength, lightweight, natural material for the production of more durable and thinner latex[20] products. There are also opportunities to develop the resin into bio-alternatives to more conventional petroleum-based polymers, including a biodegradable stretchable paper. Research is being conducted to test if the spinifex resin can be utilised to revolutionise the current $12 billion (USD) market of 3D printing and replace the reliance on conventional plastics:[21]

It is the Dreaming of the Indjalandji-Dhidhanu people and the spiritual importance of spinifex (Triodia) as a resource, which underpins all new developments into new nanotechnology research and developments. 'Increase' ceremonies are believed to have been passed down for many generations from Ancestral Beings of the Dreamtime. The function of such ceremonies was to catalyze the healthy increase or reproduction of various animal, plant, or meteorological phenomena which constitute totems in the Indigenous religious belief system, and by consequence, the total food supply. Through their ritual actions, the participants believed they connected with the Altyerre or Dreamtime dimension, and renewed a spiritual energy linking this dimension of the Ancestors with the world of mortal humans. Aspects of the travel of the Ancestral Beings were retold or re-enacted in the ceremonies through song, ritual and artworks with musical accompaniment [...] These sacred histories of Spinifex Dreaming connect or relate to the Red Kangaroo, Wild Bee, Freshwater Bream, and Black-Headed Python totems joining distant groups in the wider region. These sacred histories provide an epistemological foundation to the regional intellectual property over traditional spinifex technologies utilised for architectural, engineering, material and medicinal functions.[22]

Other examples of technological innovation can be seen in the development of watercrafts, fiberworks, message sticks, spears and woomeras, stone tools and the earliest forms of medicine, agricultural cultivation of bush plants for food, architecture and fire-stick farming for hunting and land management.

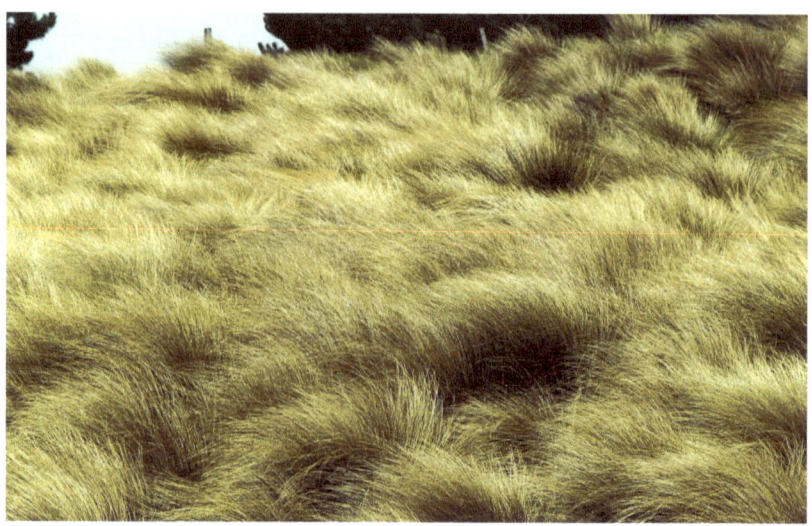

Figure 3

BEYOND IMPERIAL TOOLS

Borne out of imperialist roots, modern technologies are far from culturally neutral. For the most part, the design and development of Western technology is predicated upon the logic of extractive colonialism, whereby natural resources are drawn from the environment, regardless of associated impacts in order to control conquer and dominate worldwide economic markets. Reviewing the intention and purpose of Western technology design and development reveals its position as being *"above society both in its structure and evolution [...] seen as a source of solutions to problems that lie in society, and is rarely perceived a source of new social problems where [...] society, culture and people are required to adapt to incessant progress of disruptive technology rather than technology adapting to values of equity, participation and social and environmental sustainability."*[23]

Defining technology beyond its common, often limited, conception as an artifact of progress and/or progression of knowledge offers an opportunity to analyse its constructs through an Indigenist and feminist lens. Within Aboriginal worldview, humankind fits into, rather on top of, the land itself, shaping and forming the base teachings of Lore. From this basis, we can identify Aboriginal technologies as matricentric: flat and non-hierarchical social and cultural systems that are in symbiosis with nature itself. These are the foundational practices for Aboriginal technology creation, design and developments; extending our cognition, sense of self and consciousness, to be at one with Country, through a mutually sustaining feedback loop. Aboriginal Lore is a reciprocal law of nature, *if we do not care for Country, it dies, as do we.*

The culture of colonial and neo-liberal thinking that has driven the development of technology has led to a field of technologies that fuel inequality and unsustainable usage models. The formulation of an Indigenous-led, universal technology ethics framework requires a positioning external to the imperial and patriarchal systems which currently inform international and national policy and economic markets. Aboriginal Traditional Knowledges and governance exists within an alternate paradigm so it is imperative to firstly understand this context and the constructs that such ancient technologies have and continue to reside within. By contrasting the current drivers of new, deep technology development with their imperial and colonial states, we will see how a holistic system of governance can ensure technology development embodies the principles and practices of sustainability while ensuring universal human and environmental rights now and into the future.

Ancient technologies developed using this system are valuable in a contemporary context as they embody sustainable solutions to timely problems. There are bountiful benefits to reap from the noted cross-cultural technology practices between Aboriginal peoples, their Traditional Knowledges and pioneering historians, anthropologists, researchers and technologists bringing cultural-tech innovations into the mainstream. Spinifex is one example, but this growing awareness is evolving and transforming attitudes and perceptions, and is the basis for genuine partnerships with quantifiable socio-economic outcomes.

The custodial ethic of *Caring for Country, Caring for Kin* emphasises the importance of a deep, ecological understanding of how technologies fit into the world, suggesting a shift in focus of the design and developments of the synthetic code for deeper, more nuanced human technology inter-relationships, information sharing and knowledge transfer, and social and environmental sustainability. In this way, *Caring for Country, Caring for Kin* can inform how corporations and technologists can adopt universal strategic mandates to inform social and environmental sustainability agendas, politics, policies, initiatives and innovations.

A unique alignment of non-Indigenous technologists seeking new ways to make meaning of their work,[24] and the new wave of Indigenous technologists embracing their Traditional Knowledges to reform the foundational properties within advanced technologies is reason for optimism. These cross-cultural collaborations can do much to further new advancements in technology. Applying Pattern Thinking can refine hyper-local and contextual coding of Geospatial Information Systems (GIS) and Global Positioning Systems (GPS); mapping space and design of narrative structures to work with spatial complexities within Virtual Reality (VR) and Augmented Reality (AR); organisation of information for Information Architecture (IA); advancements in complexity systems theory for Machine Learning (ML) as part of Artificial Intelligence (AI); cradle-to-cradle approaches for advanced robotics; closed loop cycles for natural resource development and relational systems context for nanotechnologies - all for the advancement of socially and environmentally sustainable technologies: *Deep Tech*.[25]

TECHNOLOGY AS CULTURAL PRACTICE

CONCLUSION: NEW DEEP TECHNOLOGIES AND FUTURE DREAMINGS

From the cultivation of agriculture, mechanisation of labour, the information age and now, to the ubiquitous infiltration of technology, the 2nd, 3rd, and 4th revolutions have instigated shifts within social and cultural structures, impacting significantly on Western ways of seeing, being and knowing. What has eventuated is the increasing disconnection within community and a self-serving relationship to the environment. Yet, new design methodologies are responding to market demands for technologies that are socially and environmentally sustainable. Practices such as iterative design, human-centred design (HCD), circular economies, the blockchain and the sharing economy, are each affecting 'business as usual' and are driving new business models. Can these new design and development practices create conscious, spirited technologies if there is no shared story to ritualise and unite people to the places we connect with, both virtually and physically?

The patriarchal and hierarchical nature of systems design in AI developments, such as machine learning and deep learning are the basis of the dominant, contemporary human-technology interrelationships. Within these foundational systems is situated a precarious imbalance and subservient drive for human progress, inevitably at the cost of society and nature. The imperialist origins of Western technology should be further reason to caution new evolutions in AI: *deep learning, sometime referred to as machine consciousness or synthetic consciousness,*[26] where the self learning machine - intended to replicate human consciousness - is also expected to superseed human cognition and evolution. What good can come from the technology sector prophesying the rules of engagement for autonomous intelligent agents and systems designed to mimic and extend the phenomenal and cognitive evolution of consciousness when the politics for such developments are purely economic?

There is much to learn from Indigenous epistemologies and ontologies within Aboriginal Lore and its purpose to ensure technology evolution is a symbiotic process attuned to the nature of things, delicately balancing the needs of Country first, and then kin. Blackfoot philosopher, Leroy Little Bear observes: *"the human brain is a station on the radio dial, parked in one spot, it is deaf to all other stations [...] the animals, rocks, trees, simultaneously broadcasting across the whole spectrum of sentience"*[27]. In this regard, Aboriginal technology design and development processes could awaken the consciousness in technology design and expand relational experiences of time, space and mass through their interrelatedness and interconnection with all sentient beings. Through Indigenous Techno-Animism resides opportunity for Pattern Thinking to not only govern the ethics of technology development, but to inform more nuanced, complex systems for new technologies and its developmental processes.

So how do we achieve true innovation through Deep Tech developments? Through radically shifting the development process beyond the economics of imperialism at the heart of human-centred design. Our company has developed a process to resolve these issues: *Country Centered Design.*[28] The questions we pose to define the problem-space insist on cultural leadership, and both personal and collective accountability within the design process. The technology development which follows safeguards a reductionist approach by the series of questions and decisions our technologists make, informed by the protocols, rights, rituals and customs based on *Caring for Country, Caring for Kin*. In this way we curb traditional modes of technology design and software development based on self-interest, short-term gain and isolated impact. Embracing the story of the Country you are part of, to create shared intention, purpose, and meaning while breaking knowledge silos, individualism and engaging a philosophy and practice of interconnection and interrelatedness beyond the Eurocentric 'flourishing of human' to the nurturing of Country, and kin.

And what if we don't act? The increasing amplification of existing biases and prejudices; increase of data mining, loss of sovereignty and civil rights; extractive industries mining raw and precious materials with mass environmental and social impacts and increasing effects of loneliness impacting critically on the social structures of societies, communities and the health, wellbeing and life of humans. Kombumerri philosopher, Professor Mary Graham observes, "*the most basic questions for any human group, despite advances in technology, have not changed much over time; they include*:

> *How do we live together without killing each other off?*
> *How do we live without substantially damaging the environment?*
> *Why do we live?*"[30]

I propose the following three guiding principles as the first steps to develop an Indigenous Technology Ethics Framework to future-proof technology development, drawn from the Lore of this ancient Country, knowledges and stewardship of Aboriginal Elders:

1. Development of humans through sustainable environmental resources,
2. Transparency and accountability for all development practices, and
3. Technology rights equal to that of humans and the environment.

Bipartisan support from the technology sector and nation states would enable worldwide Indigenous Elders and cultural technologists to conceive, initiate and unite new Dreamings for nurtured growth and respectful and responsible development of autonomous machines, and how they reside within our society and our environment. The current imperialism within technology ethics only reinforces the human-economic center of our current social, environmental and political crises; and so, it is through an Indigenous Technology Ethics Framework we can design and build better systems and governance based on the Lore of reciprocity to grow the next generation of technologies that embody the spirit and consciousness of this land and the earth at large.

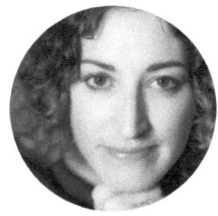

Angie Abdilla *Trawlwoolway* (Tasmanian Aboriginal), founder and CEO of Old Ways, New, leads the team of Indigenous consultants and technologists, developing social and environmental sustainability through integrated research, service and product design, and the development of deep technologies - all informed by our *old ways, new*. Angie is a Fellow of The Ethics Centre and regularly lectures on human-technology interactions and interrelationships at the University of Technology Sydney.

SHOWCASES

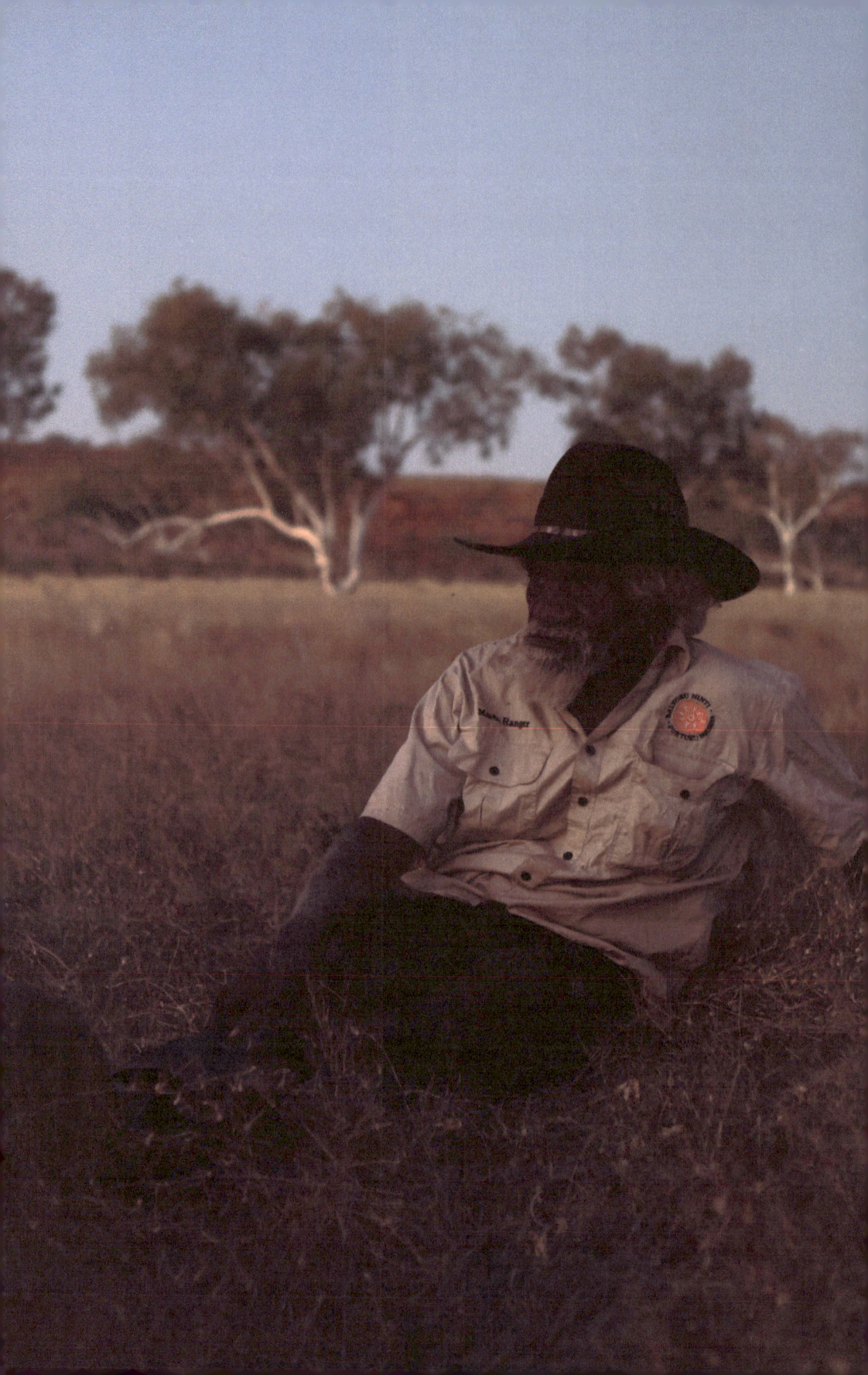

COLLISIONS
LYNETTE WALLWORTH & CURTIS TAYLOR
(360 VIDEO)

Collisions is a virtual reality journey to the land of indigenous elder Nyarri Morgan and the Martu tribe in the remote Western Australian desert. Nyarri's first contact with Western culture came in the 1950's via a dramatic collision between his traditional world view and the cutting edge of Western science and technology. 65 years later Wallworth carried cutting edge video technology into the desert so Mr. Morgan could share his story. Reflecting on the event, in this most magical of immersive experiences, Nyarri offers to viewers his experience of the impact of destructive technology and the Martu perspective on caring for the planet for future generations. Through the use of the world's most immersive technology in combination with artist Lynette Wallworth's world-class storytelling, the audience of *Collisions* is invited to experience an understanding of long term decision making via one of the world's oldest cultures.

Collisions premiered at the Sundance Film Festival and the 2016 World Economic Forum, Davos, and was awarded an Emmy Award for 'Outstanding New Approaches: Documentary'.

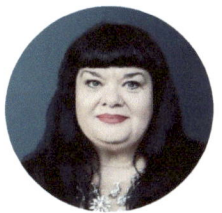

LYNETTE WALLWORTH
Artist / Filmmaker

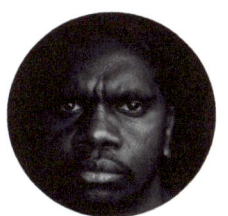

CURTIS TAYLOR
Artist / Storyteller

Lynette Wallworth is an Emmy award winning filmmaker/artist who has consistently worked with emerging media technologies. Wallworth's works include the interactive video Evolution of Fearlessness; the award winning fulldome feature Coral, with its accompanying augmented reality work; the AACTA award winning documentary Tender, and her most recent work 'Awavena' which premiered at Sundance Film Festival and was presented in competition at the Venice Film Festival. Wallworth has been awarded a UNESCO City of Film Award, the Byron Kennedy Award for Innovation and Excellence, and in 2016 she was named by Foreign Policy magazine as one of the year's 100 Leading Global Thinkers.

Curtis Taylor is a filmmaker, screen artist and a young Martu leader. Growing up in the remote Martu desert communities and in the city, Curtis has gained both tradional Martu knowledge and a Western education. Curtis was the recipient of the 2011 Western Australian Youth Art Award and Wesfarmers Youth Scholarship and his screen work has been shown in international film festivals, including the 2012 Nepal International Indigenous Film Archive Festival. Curtis is currently undertaking film and media studies at Murdoch University in Perth.

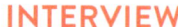

INTERVIEW

Angie Abdilla: Can you tell us about yourselves?

Curtis Taylor: Yeah. My name's Curtis Taylor. My mob is Martu, Western Desert, East Pilbara, Northwest, Western Australia. I grew up in between the desert and the salt-water. I've been lucky to learn 'both ways'. Most old people, my old people, that exile the desert towards places like Anna Plains and Liveringa, Looma, Wangkajunka Fitzroy Crossing, they're living on other people's country and had to learn their ways and their language. I've been fortunate enough to have that passed down from our people and local people from which country we reside on.

Lynette Wallworth: My family's from country New South Wales. My dad grew up in a tiny little town called Weabonga and my mum grew up in Tamworth. So most of my relatives and family are from there. My dad was a bank manager, so we moved around country New South Wales. But I was born in Sydney and I lived on and off in Sydney and my family's all around Sydney, but my relatives came from Tamworth and my Dad worked in Tamworth, Orange and he worked in Moree. We're very New South Wales based.

AA: This interview is slightly different from the rest because it's focused on your cross-cultural collaboration. Lynette, you're the lucky non-Indigenous person in the case studies primarily because, a) it's a fantastic piece of work, and b) we're really interested in how you both managed that process. Can you describe *Collisions*?

LW: Now it would be called an 'early virtual reality work'. It's a 360 [video] virtual reality experience. Fundamentally it's Nyarri's story of seeing an atomic test in the South Australian desert in the 1950s. But the work can't be separated from relationships I would say, because it emerged because of relationships.

I met Curtis at an exhibition in Fremantle [*We Don't Need a Map: A Martu experience of the Western Desert,* 2014] we were both in. This was the first work that I did with the Martu women. But it was on that first hunting trip with the Martu women that I heard that Nyarri had this story, which was the story of *Collisions*.

Collisions was set in motion by the Martu women, who invited me to be there. *Collisions* came to exist not by my own drive, but by being pulled into that work, pulled into that exhibition, meeting Curtis, hearing this story and that whole unfolding…

This whole history is all connected. Just even the fact that I was there. Because my backstory is I'd been to Maralinga in 2001 and 2002 and I had done work with the Anangu people who'd been moved off those lands. I'd gone back to the community, I'd been to Oak Valley.

Initially I had worked as a research assistant for Robert Hughes, who was in Australia working on his then-next

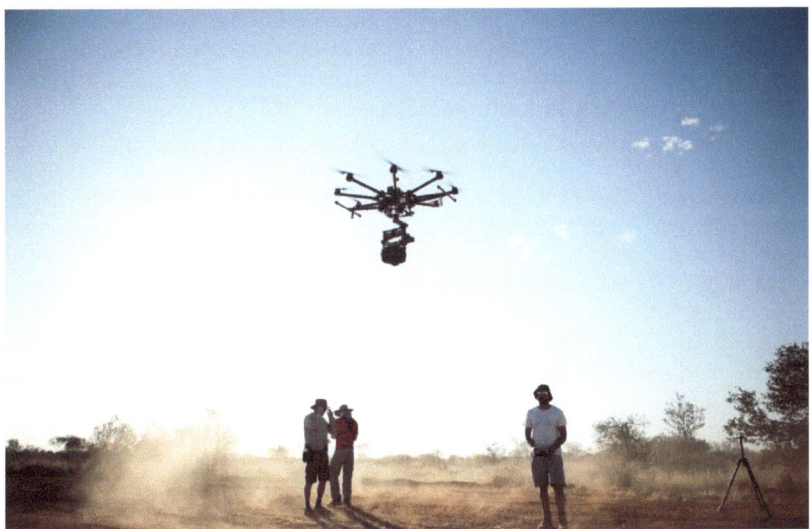

[film] series and had a car accident in WA. I was brought on because Robert was in the hospital. The Maralinga story was not going to be in the Beyond the Fatal Shore series, but I'd heard a radio program driving into the ABC for my first day at work, I heard a background briefing story about Maralinga, and I brought that story into the series.

I found a veteran who'd been a part of those nuclear tests, we filmed that veteran, and his story led me to then bring the Maralinga history into the Adelaide Festival in 2002. I worked with the Oak Valley community and they did a series of paintings about the testing that were in the 2002 Adelaide Arts Festival.

So I have these two previous relationships to this history, and not knowing any of this, I then get this out of the blue invitation to come to WA to work with the Martu women, who I'd never met before. Sitting in the desert that first night I mentioned the flowers I'd seen in the Maralinga desert. I don't know why I'd decided to talk about them, but I did. Nola, Nyarri's wife, turned to me at the fire and said "Okay, so you're going to have to talk to Nyarri." That was the beginning. It's in the very beginning of the narrations of *Collisions* which Curtis and I narrate together. The first words are: "This is not my story, this is Nyarri's story. Nyarri was waiting for me before I even met him." And that's what that refers to. Something set in motion in terms of the release of this story into the world, which Curtis can talk about more than me, to do with timing, to do with cycles of time, to do with the readiness of a story to be released, which I'm a part of. I'm just a part of that something that has been set in motion.

AA: So Curtis, how did you see this story coming into fruition? Obviously, there was a different calling for you? Can you describe what *Collisions* is for you?

CT: It's an immersive experience that takes you into Nyarri's perspective, how he saw Country and how he wanted to share his story. So you get a sense of that through the audio, his voice, and him being present on screen as himself. I think that was really powerful and well-delivered. It wasn't somebody else playing him, it was him playing himself.

I heard other Martu stories about Maralinga and Emu Fields [Nuclear testing] and knew a little bit about that story, that side. But you know, once Nyarri started to open up about his own experience... He came from the Warburton Dales area in the Gibson Desert, East of Kalgoorlie area. That's all his family's Country, so he traversed a lot of Country to end up where he is today. He held the story for a long time and was ready to share it with other community members in the Western Desert and family and other people from the region.

He opened up more as we were doing the project, as we were in production. From being out on Country and shooting it, I kept hearing more, new information about his experience. And as we went on we could see this one individual story was a part of a larger history of South Australia and I guess the world.

AA: And Lynette, what was it about Nyarri's story that captured your imagination to make a VR work?

LW: The form is really important. Nola had told me I need to speak to Nyarri and when I heard Nyarri's story, it was really like an instruction, like, that's your next job.

We were then in Parnngurr working on a second work together for the Adelaide Biennial, *Dark Heart* and the women were doing a very large collaborative painting which I was filming and that's when Nyarri came in and he and I had our very first conversation when he told me the elements of the story that he most wanted to share.

For me, that meeting was so profound, given that I had thought about this particular part of Australia's history for a long time. I asked him what it was that he thought he saw when he saw that Nuclear test. And fundamentally, his answer is the reason *Collisions* exists, because it was in that art shed that he said the words that became basically the complete heart of this work when he says "We thought it was the spirit of our gods rising up to speak with us and then we saw the spirits had made all the kangaroos fall down on the ground, as a gift to us of easy hunting...." That was such a powerful sentence, and when I heard it I realized he couldn't have thought anything else, but until I heard him say it, I never could have imagined he would have thought that.

TECHNOLOGY AS CULTURAL PRACTICE

So that of course, with this very important moment, I showed him my pictures of Maralinga, he talked to me about what he'd seen, and we also had a deeper, powerful conversation about war and violence, and the way that has been expressed through weaponry in the West, and the way that is resolved in a different way in Martu culture, or in traditional culture.

It was immediately a deep and profound and painful story there, and I asked him if he wanted to share. At the time my original thought was maybe what I should do would be another installation, because I was working on a second installation with the Martu women. I immediately had this image in my mind of Nyarri facing Oppenheimer and I felt like these two old men should meet. I felt there was a conversation there, that should have happened.

I hadn't yet seen a VR work. So at the time I heard this story I hadn't seen the form which was actually the best possible form for the work, and it wasn't until the following January that I was at Davos at the World Economic Forum showing another work, that I experienced a Virtual Reality work in a mobile headset and realized that the sense of place that it gave you, the ability for you to feel like you were not in a parallel world, but present in that world, meant that this was the form, even though it was very new and emerging, that this work should take.

I didn't know how to make that work

because I had no access to that kind of technology, but just realized at that moment this was the form the work should take. I was fortunate enough to be offered a residency with a company called Jaunt, based in Palo Alto, through New Frontiers at the Sundance Institute, that put me in a position where then I could access all that I needed in order to make the work.

AA: There's something really, quite disturbing, fascinating and disturbing about the origins of Western technology, as a cultural practice because it's so often driven by the mechanics of war. Thinking about the way in which Nyarri related and interacted with this spirit god, it's quite unnerving, and probably one of the most powerful parts of the piece for me.

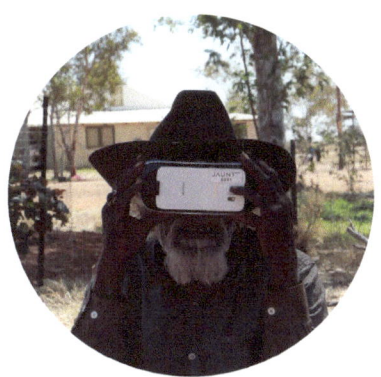

LW: It really is relevant in the sense that it's a story of the unintended consequences, of just following a technology, of allowing a technology without it being placed inside of community and culture. The scientists working on the first Nuclear tests they were actually removed from Country, they were removed from their families, they were removed from any kind of community, and they were in isolation in Los Alamos. But the proof is in that process, right? A process of deliberate disconnection, so that you're not thinking about the multiple layers or of the threads that should connect you. Curtis and I, we were working on another project with the Nyiyaparli doing some filming. We were doing research, and so we went, and remember that, Curtis, we interviewed Nyarri and he was sitting on the ground.

CT: Yeah.

LW: And we also interviewed him in a meeting that Curtis and Mia were having around the way the Martu were also trying to respond to the potential of a Uranium mine which they wanted to oppose. It's all layered. Remember that interview we had with him and then these details were emerging? Some of these details, to be honest, are not in *Collisions* because they are so disturbing that they would have distracted you from... they would have stayed in your mind in a way that would have overridden the most powerful parts of the story that Nyarri wanted to share. But we were exposed to these layers of impact - of this one event - in not just Nyarri's life - because there were also Nuclear tests in the ocean off the Western Australia coast. So the moment we open this up to discussion, you start to hear these stories which are what Curtis was

alluding to before. They were coming from more than one person.

But none of these stories, I would say, have emerged. We don't know them. They're not part of our national character. We're not holding them and we should be, because they have shaped us. So that's the importance of these stories as Curtis was saying before. It's an important, national story. It was a hidden history. And the fact that Nyarri had held it for so long and now was releasing it, at this particular moment in time, I think is why the work became as important as it did, Internationally.

CT: Yeah, and I guess most of the stuff that we found similar, when travelling with this work, was, especially in Switzerland, some of the people from some of the African countries or France or central Asia, and also in the U.S. agreed to exploit something. And these events collided with people that were living off the land, still living traditionally or still in their area, their traditional home. When they do their exploration of these minerals, a lot of people get lost and they create these things that, at the end of the day will affect you. People are living on the land and that's the main resources that they have. So yeah, there are a lot of people that we find similarities with and we talk a lot with those people that were affected by these events.

But also, coming back, when we were speaking more for Martu history, a lot of people wouldn't have been still living in the mission. Like Lynette was talking about before, they knew stories about Maralinga but I think the Montibello [Nuclear] tests were more close to home because they see the aftermath, of the fallout in the sky, coming down in the region, and they heard, so there was more close to them but also the other story about Woomera about how a group of Martu women with their children were still living in their Country and were cleared out by the Commonwealth to make way for the Woomera [Nuclear] testing and so, yeah, in the desert these *Collisions* happen between these people.

AA: There's almost something intoxicating and maddening about the practice of taking finite resources from the Earth. You know, when you see the quest for extraction through and for such destructive technologies due to unsustainable governance or regulation. I wonder what the protocols are for traditional Aboriginal technologies?

CT: Yeah, there are a lot of creation stories around the making of objects, the exploring of materials and ideas and stuff like that. I guess for us it was more, we didn't go past exploiting it fully to complete destruction, maybe in some cases they have, but yeah there's definitely stories like that, but I think a lot of people, a lot of different groups anyway, have whatever ideas they exploited to create and reshape that they didn't go past to complete destruction. As long as it feeds us and it's working, we can share this with other people. The greatest value that we have, I think is the sharing of those ideas and those ideas were shared between stories and songs and between other people and still carry on today and still reshape, rework and lot of different people are experimenting in their own different ways to exploit it to different means.

AA: Would you say that it is the intent that is the difference?

LW: Along those lines, *Collisions* has these two narrations. Myself and Curtis all the way through and there is a transitional moment in the middle of the piece in the narration, where I say "We", this is me representing Western culture; "We respond to the urgent needs of a single point in time. Martu contemplate the expanse of a hundred generations." For me this is a bridging work, trying to explain ways of being and ways of thinking that are maybe not familiar to everyone who is experiencing this work for the first time. One of the most fundamental differences was about expanses of time and contemplations of multi-generational thinking and these ideas of exploitation and consuming are completely different depending on how many generations you think about.

When we were talking to Nyarri in that moment and in Newman, interviewing him one of those first times he was sitting on the ground, and he was doing this action, Curtis, maybe you can do it, I can never do it. He was sitting on the ground and was pulling one hand behind him and he was pulling another hand forward and he was doing this circular motion. He was basically saying as these ones are leaving these ones are already

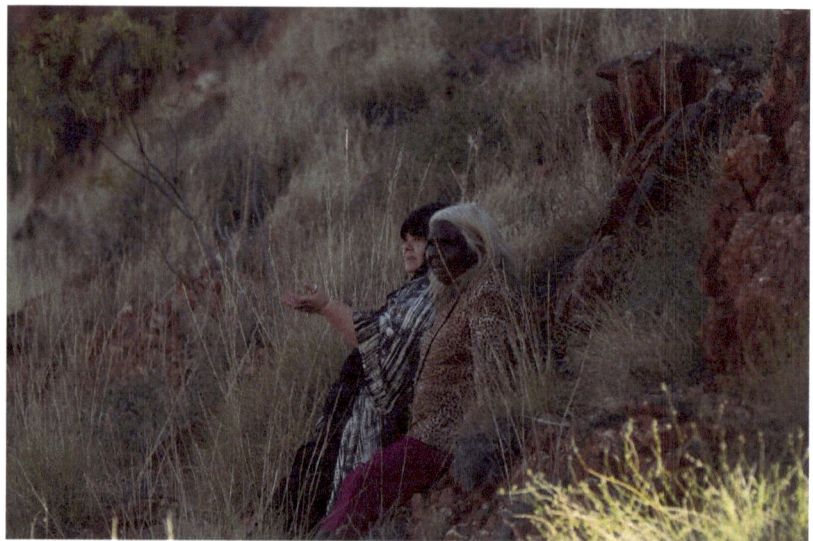

arriving and the way of thinking which is held inside of this work is about that. And of course if your thinking is about not just this current moment and that's what I was thinking about in terms of where this work was going, where it was going to land and who was going to first see it in terms of world leaders and heads of industry was about how can you help those people think beyond this current moment in time and this multi-multi-generational thinking which is at the heart of any First Nation's thinking.

I've been into the libraries in Canberra. I've seen the letter that King George III wrote to James Cook. I've looked at that letter and you know what that letter says? The first commision was to observe the Transit of Venus in Tahiti and then the second letter, the secret commission, was to go and search for the Great South Land to see if there

are any mines, minerals or resources. That's in the very first letter written to James Cook for the British exploration of this country. The idea of consuming was there, of consuming and taking and capitalizing was there from the beginning. So there's two mindsets inside this work which is why it is the way it is. It's trying to hold those threads and place them side by side.

Josh Harle: Thinking about your intended audience, it sounds like an important goal of *Collisions* was giving a non-Indigenous audience, the politicians at Davos for example, contact with an Indigenous worldview.

LW: Yes. Nyarri in terms of his own vision, was very focused on parliament here in Canberra. He was interested always, in getting in front of politicians. He used to list cities, you know Sydney, Canberra. He also was passionately interested in leadership, political leadership. He is political in nature. So that time when we were in Newman and having these meetings, I put a PowerPoint together about what it looked like to go to Davos. I had pictures from the World Economic Forum, and we showed PowerPoint, which was like these pictures of Kofi Annan and Bill Clinton. It was like foregrounding, "Are these the people you want to take the story to"? And yes, he did and later, at Davos, Curtis had his photo taken with Kofi Annan, so we could update the powerpoint, with this changed reality of the story having now travelled into that Intended world.

I think the power of an artwork is a different thought in motion. And these are mostly forms of power. We had the opportunity of a new form with a powerful story that could be placed in front of people who, should they decide to make a different decision, can create far reaching impact.

But interestingly, when I started to try and get the funds for it, a lot of people said to me "While the Nuclear issue is interesting from a historical point of view, it's not relevant, it's not contemporary". So that was, if you can imagine early 2015. And it's true, at the time, in 2015, people were not thinking that there was going to be a ramping of the Nuclear threat. So again, there's something kind of prescient in the timing of the release of this work, of this story, that has to do with Nyarri's instinct.

AA: I think *Collisions* is definitely one of the first, most successful creative adaptions of the VR format. How did you work with international developers in post-production, and how did Terri Janke's Indigenous Cultural Intellectual Property (ICIP) protocols inform your process?

LW: Because it was new and those protocols are not in place. One, around what should be contained in the work in this form, given that the form makes you feel present in that Country. So, the work itself holds the kind of protocols of a meeting, that apply to me to go there. In the work itself, you're told where you are travelling and why you are travelling. You are told you are going to Nyarri's home, where he lives, and it's a story he wants to share. And then you hear him singing, then you meet him, he comes and greets you. So, you're first invited and you are welcomed. There's a form of protocols of the meeting, and travelling to that community, that are built into the experience of the work.

And secondly, there was a question of, given that I was working with a US-based residency, how would the cultural protocols be applied to all layers of the work. That needed to be contractually enforced. So, I went to Terri and asked her to draft a contract to protect Nyarri's intellectual and cultural property rights. And so she drafted a contract, which then I had to sign. When we took it to the community, Curtis read it to him, but the contract was basically to protect his rights, and I was adhering to them.

His rights in relation to the work. And what that contract then enabled me to do, was enforce those rights with anyone else that I had to enter into contract with to make the work.

Everything had to be very carefully navigated so that we could always come back to the organic protection of this being Nyarri's story and that that could never be lost. His cultural rights within the work could never be lost. So, that ended up, that's not an easy thing I have to say to you, to navigate. With lawyers, the lawyer we were working with who worked for Jaunt, he used to be the lawyer for George Lucas. We are talking heavy hitter, that level. My producer Nicole Newnham was dealing with this stuff, and I would be on Skype a lot of the time with her as she was battling it out. But actually, the benefit of working a new form is you can also say, "I know this isn't traditionally done, but this is a new form, so let's do it. Let's do this differently. Let's create a new pathway."

Because we are working with this new technology, there certainly was no pathway of how to make the work. There was also no pathway in terms of those structures that you might want to put in place around the way the rights were held in the work, or any potential revenue share for such a work.

So, Nicole and I would continually push back in that way, guided by Terri and those pathways to protocol that she had developed for Screen Australia. So it was down to these

things, and a lot of the time people would fight us on them. And I could always say, "Yeah but, however, if you don't agree to this you'll put me in breach of my contract". So we could enforce things, and it's like procedural I guess, it's contractual, but somehow there was something very satisfying about trying to shift this new form to to acknowledge these agreements which we had entered in to. In order to be able to make the work.

So, even in the copyright, if you look at the copyright, right at the end of "*Collisions*", it'll say, "Copyright to me from a story by Nyarri Morgan".

Our lawyer said at the time, "Well you don't need to acknowledge Nyarri's story again here in the copyright at the end because you're contractually acknowledging that, and you've adhered to all of that".

And I said, "But, is there anything to stop me acknowledging it?"

And she said, "No".

And I said, "So let's put it in".

So we learned a tremendous amount about pushing back beyond the "legalese", the kind of existing parameters of the way things are done. And saying "Well, I don't care how they were done before. Can we do this?" That was often where the greatest exhaustion came for Nicole and I. But now I feel like a lot of the satisfaction came because we were able to shape the process, that worked for us all and in the end it was satisfying for us all.

JH: I really like the thinking that for VR, as an immersive medium, it requires people in the community to agree to the visit, to welcome people into the community as part of that process. I think it's really important to take seriously what comes along with a medium. Not just take it on face value, but to say absolutely this is the significance.

LW: Also to take ethical responsibility for the fact that you, if you're pioneering in a form, you're creating a track. So why not deeply, deeply consider what might be the ways that I can mirror a relationship. One, I only go to this community because I'm invited. So that is at the beginning of *Collisions* as well, you're told you're being carried there, you're invited to go. And secondly, I don't leave you there. Maybe that seems like a small thing, but at the end, there's a drone that goes up, and you're lifted up. And then it's just Nyarri walking on the ground below, and you're actually lifted into the sky. Into the blue. And then there's a final kind of moment, like an epilogue I guess, where Nyarri is just sitting, painting. But in terms of the narration of the work, you are lifted up and out. It's appropriate because VR is a powerful form, it does make you feel present, therefore you needed to be lifted back out at the end. This is a not a place where you can stay.

And you have people like Mark Zuckerberg saying that VR means you can go anywhere and do anything. I wanted to place protocols of meeting inside this work, given that it is, by its very nature, a bridging work. It's a work with two narrators, one indigenous and one non-indigenous. Around two histories, one known and one unknown. And it needed all of the time to respond to the protocols in the community so that it didn't exploit the visitor's presence.

So for using the VR and the drone, we held a community meeting as soon as we got there, everyone came to the meeting, put the headset on, and saw what the form could reveal. And then, we were guided continually about, for example, even how high a drone could go. Because of people's ability to actually know what it would see behind or in front, and what couldn't be seen. And there was not a shot we took that we had to remove because it revealed something it shouldn't, because they were in control all the time, of what was visible.

AA: What a great process. I think it's the reason why the work is so rich and has such reverence. When creative works embody such a respectful process, it becomes evident, and the story is better for it. The protocols are really beneficial in guiding how you care for and tell a story properly.

LW: I think it's kind of beholden on us to think about that when the technology's new. You actually get to consider what this process should be, and how might this process be, and as I said we have enough of a relationship between us to actually carve that out together, to map that out together. And that, for me, is one of the layers of the beauty of *Collisions* is that it held all of that thinking inside of it.

AA: I really liked the way the narration works with Nyarri speaking in language. Was this a creative or technical decision to embed the interpretation within your narration?

LW: Well, Nyarri wanted to speak English, didn't he, Curtis?

CT: Yeah. He wanted to speak English, but the things weren't translating across, so we said, "Don't worry about speaking English, just speak Martu Wangka and we'll fix it up, translate it; how you're saying it right now, or what you're trying to get across.

LW: He's addressing the camera a lot, and for 360 VR, wherever the camera is, the viewer, the visitor feels themself to be. And so, Nyarri would say, "Where's the Europe person?" And I'd say, "The Europe person is going to be where that camera is." And then he would talk. But he speaks how many different languages, Curtis? Seven languages?

CT: Seven, yeah.

LW: And often he had really specific things he wanted to say. We had an audio recordist with us, Liam Egan, who's worked with us before on another project. So we did some recordings which were just audio, so that we could really get the elements of this story that Nyarri wanted to convey, and then when I was in Berkeley, Curtis translated the audio, and then we could work on piecing

parts of it together. It was a long process to get Nyarri's words as he wanted them said, and then to add the narration on top of that, but it was essential, because right from the start there was certain really particular things that he wanted to express. And as Curtis said, he so wanted to express them to the 'Europe people' where he imagined the work was going to be seen, that he tried to say them in English. And so it was important to actually have his words there and have the translation sitting under them, which Curtis did, so that nothing was missed.

AA: Was there any directorial consideration in the post production on how you wove those three different elements together? Because it's three different types of storytelling, there's Nyarri's voice in language, there's the transcription, and then there's narration. There's pivotal points in the story that Nyarri was really clear about wanting to address those 'Europe people', did you use that as the basis for your direction?

LW: There was a very important scene, the scene where Nyarri is at the fire, he was looking directly at the camera and talking directly to the camera saying the things he most wanted to say. Putting the work together, those words worked more powerfully at the end of the film, because they were so significant. They're actually what we're left with. In terms of where they were shot, they were scenes where he was talking, and he was saying, "Look after your Country, look after your young ones, think about the land

and the ones to follow." That ends up being what we're left with. We see him far below us tending the land through fire, walking about. When I mention that moment where we're lifting off, we're above, and he's on the ground, and he's giving these instructions, that ends up being the very last thing that he says to us. But really, it wasn't in direction in terms of in-the-field, it was in putting the work together through the very long edit that things, as they do, became clearer. This short 17 minute work had almost three months of post production to shape it into the piece it became and through that process the most powerful expression of the work became clear. So in terms of message it was simply "This is going to be more impactful in terms of Nyarri's message, if it's placed here rather than there."

JH: Can you speak more about how working in VR affected your activities as a director?

LW: Well, those considerations around the protocols, the showing, the traveling, and having the greeting, and the leaving, were all built into the work because of the intimacy of the form. As were the presentation decisions for *Collisions*. Nicole and I strove to have sychronised screenings of *Collisions* right from the very first presentation in order that experiences of the work were communal. Again that was a push on the technology as was currently available - we worked with *Two Bit Circus* so that we could deliver sychronised screenings, so the work could be experienced as a collective dream, so the first

screening, from Davos onward, were collective. In terms of direction in post, you use sound a lot more to call people's attention to where you want to go in VR. It's an incredibly valuable directorial tool in a 360 space. We record it spatially.

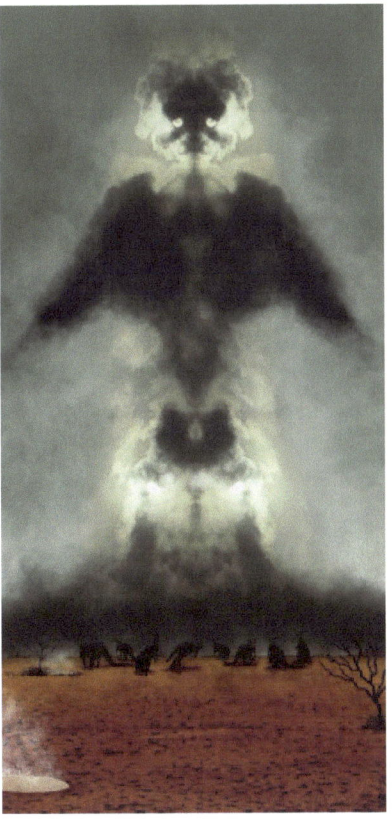

I had created a storyboard of twenty shots that I went through with Nyarri before we began, but we were being informed by where Nyarri felt things should happen in terms of all those shots. So if you think about that scene where he's singing, we were all climbing up one area, and Nyarri just went off and scrambled up to another point. And he was like, "No, this is the best spot here." Often it was about what could and could not be seen in relation to the country from the point of view of the 360 camera.

CT: Yeah, it was good. We had the end of some nights that we could see some of the rushes [the raw footage], just for some of the Elders in the community to see if there wasn't anything shown that wasn't allowed to be seen by the public. They were wherever we went, the placement of the camera. Nyarri knew where to place it. He had this spatial awareness, already, what would be blocked out or "what I want people to see and what I don't want people to see", whether it be ridges and rocks and things blocking out the stuff that were really close by and couldn't be captured on film.

AA: Curtis, were there different protocols and considerations, from film to this new experimental format of VR? Were you advising the community around the process in the same way that you would within the film?

CT: I think that most of them were advising us at the end, when they saw the rushes, "Oh, can I have a look?" When we shot at the rock, they swiveled around and made sure everything was clear, and then they said, "Oh, okay, that's good." And even the first shot where you're coming into the community and we're flying up above them. You

don't realize, after when they saw the camera, that they said, "Maybe when you cut it or next time you put the camera in the air, just fly higher. Make sure you come up to this level."

LW: Even in the scene when Nyarri walks up to the Oppenheimer camera, you see the community sitting there, and there's a lot of people sitting around. Even where people place their chairs in relation to one another was according to where they needed to be. There was a continual rearrangement or organization according to protocols. Even when Nyarri was sitting in relation to Muuki, he had worked it out.

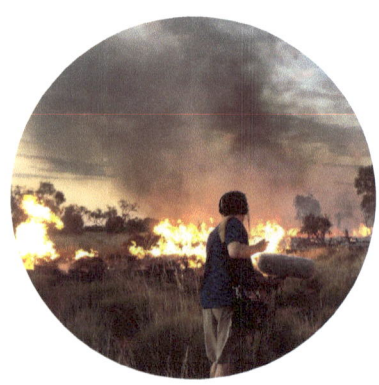

CT: Yeah, even where people were placed, I think that was pretty normal where they placed themselves, sitting down in a social setting. People knew where to sit down and stuff like that. And there were times where they'd say, "Maybe this would work better if you sit down over here." It just looked different, made it work for the camera.

AA: Did you relate to VR differently due to the history of Indigenous storytelling being circular and spatially grounded in Country? There's quite a difference to film, it's frame and the Western three-act story structure. Did you find that challenging, or was that a creative opportunity?

LW: Well I come from installation art, so it's non-linear. It's not a three-act structure. It's creating a space where something can unfold. You create such a space so that the viewer might enter at any point and still be able to find the meaning within the work. It's not structured in that filmic way where you're pushing people through a linear narrative. *Collisions* does have a linear narrative, but certainly the habit or the experience of working in installation is a natural fit for virtual reality, and for this kind of oral history storytelling. Installation informs a habit of helping to guide people to act in a way that feels instinctively right, and if I hit that correctly then the work will flow.

AA: Do you think it's the conventions within filmmaking that drove the lineal aspects of *Collisions*? I noted you do use filmic conventions to guide the audience's attention and the story's direction, for example, how the camera is placed, editing and sound design in post production. It certainly feels like you're being guided through the story as opposed to a lot of other VR experiences which enable the participant as an active agent.

LW: That's something to do partly with the invitation from Sundance New Frontiers to take up the residency. Part of the invitation was, in those early days, to see whether it was actually possible to follow a complete narrative in VR. Because a lot of the works that existed in 2015 were 'experiences' as opposed to narratives. Sundance particularly chose artists for the residencies who they felt might be able to experiment with narrative form within that new technology.

And even the filmic considerations that you're talking about were really part of the residency parameters as well - in terms of a challenge to push this new form forward. Because at that point, people weren't even doing filmic transitions within VR. People were fading down to black and fading up from black in order to move you from one scene to another. There was a lot of pressure to keep doing that. There were conditions told to me, at the beginning, which were a series of rules that I was told, if I broke them, people wouldn't take in the work, that the experience would be too jarring. And that was, "it can't be longer than 10 minutes", "you have to fade in and out of scenes", "you can't move the camera". It was a whole series of things which, well actually, we broke every single one of them.

But at the time that was the belief. I showed some of the raw footage to Joe Bini, who's Werner Herzog's editor, who was an advisor on the narration. I wanted to have someone who had a tradition of helping to do narration, because I've never done

TECHNOLOGY AS CULTURAL PRACTICE

narration before, and I showed him this early footage, and I was saying, "These are the things people are saying." And he said, "That's what people said at the beginning of film." You can't move the camera, you can't get a close up, you can't do this, you can't do that. And he said, "Do it all." So actually it was about trying to work out, could we do these things? Because we hadn't seen them done. They hadn't been done.

JH: It sounds like you said earlier about a bridge between two ways of thinking. Part of that was between film and spatial narrative, and also working with people who are experts in a spatial storytelling. And obviously there's a bit of frisson at the point that, if you're breaking rules, then you're doing good things, for sure. It seems like ideas of spatial storytelling have been brought closer to film.

LW: Curtis can say more about this, but I feel like part of these stories can't really be told unless it can be attached to place, and that's what this form makes possible.

CT: We couldn't film where it happened, on site, but we cheated in the landscape, we could have access to Nyarri and the landscape around, we didn't have to travel far. It wasn't shot in South Australia, in northwest Pilbara in Western Australia. It was easy to get access to. For us having access to these places, whether they be in the riverbed or in between these flood plains with these hills surrounding and the top of the rock wall which had an escarpment on top

of that, all of these different places that were showing the diversity of the landscape and different parts of the story, how they work well with parts of the narration and what Nyarri was conveying at the time when he was singing throughout the experience. That was really important, so at the start, having that ... It became, and it is a character within itself, Country.

AA: When Nyarri is singing, is he singing up Country?

CT: Well, yeah, that song was composed at the mission, but it was a song about clouds forming and the rain coming. There were these other stories that were brought in from other people, other places that matched this and fitted it.

I guess one of the most fun moments for me was at ACMI, and we were singing, doing a Welcome, and had the mob from Melbourne come along, to do the welcome for us, kind of prompting Nyarri, "you should do a different song for this one." He chose a song about this lady's journey where she lived on the mission in Geelong, went along with church fellows from Fremantle, and then was on a boat to England, crossing the sea. A lot of people back home on the mission were worried about her and they composed this song about her, a contemporary song, a story, and yeah it was really fitting for Nyarri to pick that song at that time for the opening at ACMI.

LW: I think it was beautiful, because he sang this song about this woman who traveled by boat to the UK, and they made this song about that journey and Nyarri had really wanted the work to go to London, which it did. (It's going to the Barbican next year, so it will be in the UK again actually, so it's keeping on moving). But I think he said when he was at ACMI he sang that particular song because *Collisions* had become the next part of that traveling. It's his story, and that story's traveled to England in this form.

AA: That's powerful.

LW: It was an amazing moment. It was like the song continuing.

CT: Yeah, and coming back to that directorial role, *Collisions* has a kind of narrative in this, with the sound and with certain triggers surrounding the experience, wanting people to engage with this space within the experience. But also, every time people watch it, they're directing themselves, every time they watch it, there's a difference, that they in a sense are directing themselves, directing their own experiences.

JH: Can you talk more about the soundscape and sound design in VR?

LW: Well we had Dolby Atmos sound, so we recorded spatially, and we also had lapel mics. We didn't have a sophisticated camera, we had a very early model that Jaunt had which was 16 GoPros, so it was before their bespoke models like the Neo. So we had a couple of different spatial mics in addition and then lapel mics, and then one of the really helpful things,

was that we had an earpiece Nyarri could wear. One of the big challenges with 360 VR, with the sound, is that we can't be visible in the scene, you've got to be hidden. He's walking about and we're behind a tree or behind the truck. So he can't see us. It's awkward for him. But we had an earpiece which meant he could hear Curtis talking to him, or we could be talking to him as he's walking. So he was not alone.

So there were just little things that we used that were very helpful filming in that space, but afterwards, Dolby wrote code to bring the sound in. So we could get this version of Dolby that's in VR. Curtis was with us at the time because we were recording the narration at Skywalker Sound, and that was really great. Because they're Skywalker Sound, they had all these sounds, but one of the important things was that we needed the sound of a dying kangaroo. And they said, "Yeah, well we'll have something like that." But of course they didn't have that particular sound. So Curtis contributed that to Skywalker Sound.

Also then we would go from there to the animation place, where the people were working on the animation, and same sort of things. I had worked over weeks to get the animations as I wanted them in terms of movement and action but they had the color of the kangaroos wrong.

So Curtis was giving very particular instruction about what the kangaroos would sound like, the kangaroos' colour, which was awesome. Because there were teams of people by this

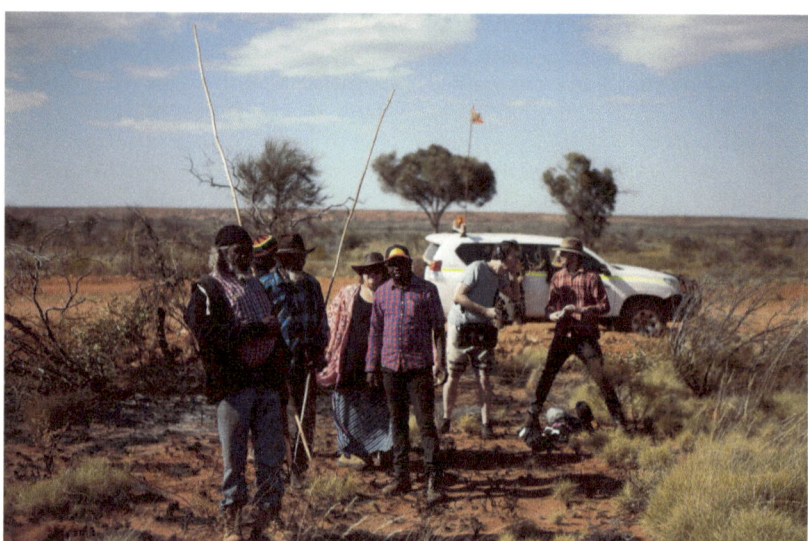

stage that we were working with in order to pull everything together.

The wonderful thing about the sound, the Dolby Atmos is that it responded to where you looked. So, if you looked up, you heard it more clearly. If you looked down, you heard it so distinctly. So it is immersive in that way. And so it really kind of adds a whole other layer. It enriches the sense of your immersion in that space.

So Liam bought his first VR mic. He was obsessed with going out, making Curtis shoot off guns so that he could get particular sounds. It was a very rich, spatial palate he provided.

Then that's where Curtis and I recorded our narration. Do you want to tell the story about the Martu effect of the technology, both you and Nyarri, Curtis?

CT: Yeah, some of the cameras didn't work. Some nights that we shot, some of the cameras didn't work so that we'd shoot it again. They stretched some of the images out so that they could fill in the space. In the recording studio, I think our first recording we did was lost, I don't know, something happened and then we had to go back, do it again.

LW: It was very specific. *Collisions* was shot with 360 3D, which with 3D means you can't put the camera closer than like a metre to, say if it was the person that you were filming, because otherwise you're not going to be able to stitch those two cameras together that are providing the stereo.

The closest we could ever get the camera to Nyarri, in terms of close up shots, would be a metre, but you have a trigger that would trigger off all of the 16 cameras at once. Otherwise it's a nightmare in terms of stitching all of that content together at that point, with the facilities available for stitching, it just became very difficult.

I think it was two or three nights in where the DP from Palo Alto came to me and said, "Is there something powerful about him?" Because whenever they put the camera within a metre of him, the cameras facing him would not trigger. So this came to be called the Nyarri effect.

They would have to go in and manually trigger off those cameras that were nearest to him, which was irritating, but also, by the end, we were all used to it. That was just what was happening.

Then we traveled all the way to Skywalker Sound, and Curtis did his narration. And the narration did not take, so we had to do the narration all over again. A combination of technologies and resonances.

JH: As a side note, the Dolby Atmos 3D tools you helped create are now available for VR for free.

LW: It was an interesting time because you had people like Dolby, like Skywalker Sound wanting the experience of the post-production process in order to build the tools that we're now probably all using.

It's the benefit of pioneering in that way, being there first, I feel like you have a greater freedom to push and see what's possible. But you're also dealing with things when they're not quite ready. So actually, it was a lot of time that Dolby guy writing the code while we were on the sound stage. It was quite stressful but ultimately so wonderful to experience the result.

I think a good way to think about doing this sort of work is that you're making a path for other people to come after you, which is why it matters how you think about everything you're doing.

JH: It's very exciting to think that a creative project is driving the development of technology, that the code is being written in response to the creative project rather than the creative project having to deal with whatever's built into what you're given.

AA: Has *Collisions* informed this work you're doing now? What sort of medium are you working in?

CT: It's all like painting, sculpture in mainly wood. So, yeah, that's the kind of medium I've been working on since I moved away from video and just work with my hands more. I've been working with more wood materials and metal and other stuff, and painting. I haven't painted for a long time.

I started out painting. Telling stories and making films was taking a lot of my time. So, it's good to come back to this medium and see where I'm at and still experiment with ideas and stories, different techniques. So, yeah, that's really exciting for me.

Most of the time I'm not collaborating with anybody else, I'm just on my own, and I find it really peaceful doing that. But also in a weird way, I'm still telling stories. Not my stories, but my grandfather's stories, my dad's dad, he passed away. But I'm telling his stories, stories that he composed, songs that he composed when he was alive. He was a really good composer of stories and songs and dance, and that's the stories. In a weird way, I'm collaborating with this work, with his stories. But, yeah, I was always interested in other ideas and the world outside the Western Desert and that kind of modern Western Desert thinking.

My first collaboration was with Lily Hibberd. She's based in Paris now, but we had been telling stories about phone booths and how they arrived into the communities and what the people in the communities were thinking about it and how they were utilizing them and how they still utilize them. But now, even though most of the Country has mobile reception, there are a few communities that don't have that network connection. So, yeah, it's still being used in that way. That was my first collaboration with somebody else and it was really exciting. I learned a lot from that and I learned a lot from *Collisions*, working with Lynette and with all the team.

AA: And, Lynette, how is your work now changed from *Collisions* to the project you're working on now?

LW: It happened as a really direct link. I really think it's important to say, if

we're talking about collaborations, that Curtis' role is really particular. So much of this work, there's no rule book for it. My feeling is it has to be based on real relationship and trust and that you can't shortcut that. For me, the relationship with Curtis is extremely important. In a way, I can't even properly explain it. There's no comparable relationship to this one in the sense that I simply couldn't have done this work without him. It wouldn't be able to exist. I wouldn't be able to make it. I wouldn't be able to show it.

That's why I call it a bridging work. I don't even think we have the language for what this kind of melding is that has to happen. I'm not able to go to the place of making this work except that Curtis is standing beside me and in such a way that I am free to do what I can do. I was free to fulfill the part of it that was mine to do. It's respect and trust from a position of humility. I'm entering into something which, even though it's an invitation to me, there are levels of responsibility that Curtis is bearing on my behalf because I do not understand them. There's a part of me that's conscious and aware of that, as much as I can be conscious and aware, and trying not to mess up or overstep or make a mistake. But there's a part of me that knows all of the time that at any minute I might and that, if I do, that doesn't fall to me, that would fall more heavily on him. It's why the relationship is so incredibly important. I can't overstate what it means to me and that it's a real thing.

So, *Collisions*, and that process, this is like the third work I did with the Martu, but I struggle for the words to say what that means. I can explain it to you as a feeling and a sensation. I can tell it to you as the knowledge, which I don't have in any other part of my professional life of this person taking the role of standing beside me in order that I am enabled to fulfil what I'm undertaking. So, that's incredibly meaningful.

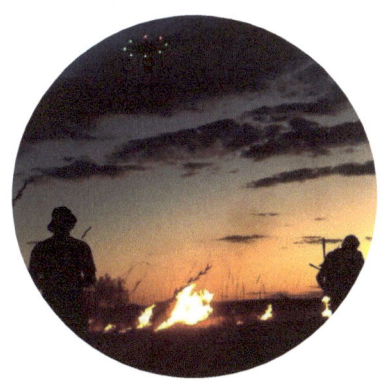

I think, in part, that's why the work was able to fly in the way it did once it entered the world because everything was done in the right way. So, one of the moments of showing *Collisions*, was when it was seen by an Amazonian chief Tashka Yawanawá - [Chief of the Yawanawá people in Acre, Brazil] who saw in it not just the potential for the technology to work well, but that the process would work well for his own community. So he then invited me to come to the Amazon to create the next work which is called *Awavena*. And the two works are very, very much related.

The dream we had with it was that Curtis and Nola might be able to travel to the Amazon or *Awavena* might be able to travel here. Now I think we might virtually make that happen. They should meet one another. But, in a sense, if you can imagine, there's a culmination that's happening in these works where they're speaking to one another. Even though they're from a different part of the world and the stories are different, the works are talking directly to one another. That one work has led to the next so those relationships should be fostered as well.

AA: He's an inspiring man, Tashka.

LW: And he loves new technology and saw the potential in it, experiencing *Collisions*, but also felt our process working with the community, and so could extend the invitation. And *Awavena* will lead to other works. Tashka talks about himself as a bridge. He has a different sort of history that has led to him trying to navigate the two worlds [Western and Indigenous] also, through technology.

AA: Would you say that that's the capacity of technology or is it because of its emergent state and your combined ability to create a solid respectful process to navigate and utilise the technologies? Is it the tool or is it actually the process?

LW: It's something that I think would bear more thinking. I have a limited, at the moment, way of speaking about it. But if you talk about a visioning technology that we have built and show it to peoples who have traditionally practiced different visioning technologies — the ability to leave the body and move and see and travel — so for the Yawanawá, Tashka saw that alignment very clearly. He said, "Oh, this acts like medicine." It opens a portal. It carries you without your body to a place you haven't been. It intensifies color and sound. You meet the Elders, you're given a message and then you return. We can show you something of this because that's what our visioning does. So they wanted, in a way, to co-opt the technology to demonstrate the practice of visioning.

I think if you accept, and I do accept, that there are different ways of being, that we have evolved according to traditions and cultural practices and if there is a technology that can allow us to have a sense of a different way of perceiving this reality then, for me, that's a beneficial process. So, I'm very open to, and was very open to, the Yawanawá request to use the technology, to say this is the way we see the world. And the base of that, I think, is completely aligned with *Collisions* with Martu, because when I said to the Yawanawá, "Well, tell me fundamentally then what this vision should show.", they said, "That everything is alive." So use the technology to show everything being alive.

AA: Curtis, do you feel like *Collisions* is, at its heart, a film or is it...How do you describe it? How do you relate to it?

CT: More of an experience. But then again, I didn't really ask that question myself, but I kept asking other people and a lot of different people would come up with different answers. Whatever they took out of being in that experience, that was theirs and theirs alone. That's all that mattered to me. But how I see it is, yeah, an experience. Even being kind of deprived from going back home, living in your homeland, and I get to see these landscapes and stuff through *Collisions* because I live in Perth in the city and I don't really have the opportunity to travel up there. I can experience the landscape and the people and stuff like that. I see it as an experience. It's also drama with the Martu story-telling that lies within this experience.

JH: That's really interesting. Do you use it often as a way of going back and visiting?

CT: Yeah, whenever I feel that I need to reconnect in someway, some levels. That's sort of enjoyment and fulfillment to me when I get to put the headset on them I just do, again its different to being on the phone and you're talking to another person on the end of the line, I guess you can experience it, the place at the time.

AA: It's really exciting to know that innate connection to Country is possible through VR.

LW: We talked about, say sometimes when the old people have to go away when they have dialysis and they can't stay, the community VR as a way of being able to feel that they're back walking around. It would be great from that kind of perspective to give that sense of place.

CT: Those are the talks that came out during the time. Show *Collisions* across Australia. We are going to go into places like hospitals or nursing homes where people are there, maybe they're getting old and cannot go back and forth at least so, be there virtually and hopefully that's good enough for them.

LW: Other people that have seen it are mining companies for showing to their staff right?

CT: Yeah to their staff. A lot of people from all kind of discipline, walks of life, seen this, and we showed it to them, hungry and interested, sharing it whether they be in the workplace or their friends and stuff like that. Yeah, it's exciting, yeah.

AA: Curtis, you mentioned you work across a number of different formats and genres. How do you feel these different practices have informed your ability to work in 360?

CT: That all kind of went out the door with me working mainly sculptural, and film I guess. For us when we tell our stories, reimagine our stories, tell our stories again around the campfire but also do our Ceremonies, we are visiting places with song, but also people have the power to transport themselves and we call it '*kapukurryi*' where you're leaving your body to transport yourself, your soul and you,

even though you're in a dream state that's real because you come back.

Once you come back you have memory of things that you didn't have before and things that maybe were lost that you're maybe trying to reveal or trying to get knowledge of. So *kapukurryi* is a state where that happens when in a sense you can teleport to another time and place and that you'll see you have these experiences which are more spatial. *Karninyijarra* right down on the ground, subterranean level that we are now in the landscape to, went over to the sky and beyond.

Those are the places that these songs and stories hold. Even though when we were filming at the cave, that's the scene where Nyarri's singing, on the other side some really special places that, I was alluding to that before, but people were wanting to see the rushes of them, saying, "Okay, that's hidden, that's good you're cleared to use that shot, but next time don't do that area because of so and so." Even though paintings that these artists do in the Western Desert look like linear landscapes, like it's flat, it's not. Its spatial, it's telling a story of underground, all the different levels and 360 from all of the vegetation, rock, river, and all the place-names they may have walked through that people told them stories or they had experience of *kapukurryi*. They tell those stories in this format by painting. It wasn't new territory for us, whether we would place the camera here and what we see. A lot of people would definitely leave where they are, their body. They go and also see 360,

TECHNOLOGY AS CULTURAL PRACTICE

like how the camera would see it and that's what we make sure.

LW: So I insisted on the drone even though it was a big expense for us to have that big drone there for the reason Curtis is saying. It was essential that the camera could see the way people can see. The way the Martu see. From this level on the ground and below the ground but also from that level, high above it.

The work wouldn't have been right if it didn't have that way of seeing. So, we worked hard to bring a drone in there and be able to have that perspective but also what Curtis is saying about this way of experiencing something which is a dream, which is a real thing, but happening in a dream state is why I think the technology is particularly powerful at this moment in time. I don't know if it will always have the same effect, but at the moment if we observe in terms of people's brain activity, where they're recalling a virtual reality experience they are recalling it as though it was a dream. They're not recalling it as though it was a film, as in something I watched, that I saw, but didn't happen to me. We are recalling it as though it somehow did happen to me. I know it wasn't real as in this reality, but it was real in another realm, which is why I think these alignments are working around these states. That state that Curtis just described to you is a practice of the Martu and the potential for that state to be activated or simulated in someway maybe it can help us understand each other. So I'm interested in this time where

the VR experience for the moment, we haven't codified it yet as separate.

That's why this is a powerful moment for powerful storytelling.

AA: I think another layer to the reason why *Collisions* is so powerful is because it is Country guiding you all along the way in the creation of that story. It's quite a different process to filmmaking, right?

CT: Yeah. That's why a lot of the other old people from the community really wanted see the rushes because they wanted to make sure that it was clear and have us respect them. But also the crew was, you had Nyarri, Nola, and me so we lived in the area, we knew the Country where we shot and we knew which area was okay and safe to shoot. We were respecting, making sure we put that respect into Country, but yeah… Lynette was directing and making sure her vision she wanted and envisaged was being shot, taking down the images and stuff like that but also you had the DOP [Director of Photography], the camera-person also.

JH: Are there any Indigenous projects from others you'd like to mention, storytelling using technology?

CT: There's definitely projects worth checking out like *Love Punks* [2016 iPad-based interactive graphic novel created for NEOMAD with Stewart Campbell] up in Roebourne with the kids up there, and *Thalu*, which Tyson Mowarin did.

LW: I think Mikaela Jade's doing really interesting stuff with *InDigital*, because she's working in community, working with AR and they're building apps, and so I'm super excited at what is going to emerge from the work she's doing. The good thing is now the funding bodies are funding VR.

The benefit of doing *Collisions* is that it opened a lot of doors and meant I could go into the funding bodies and talk to them about funding this form.

I think the wonderful thing is that we have government funding here and this opportunity for innovation in VR now. *Collisions* winning an Emmy was hugely beneficial and significant. That a VR work won that award, a news and documentary award, meant people took VR seriously. It's helped VR's credibility and that all goes towards assisting the funds coming towards it so that more works can happen. The big thing is always going to be access to such swiftly emerging technology and that's the ongoing challenge. How do we foster the sort of residency I benefited from, with people who've got the technology which is cutting edge? You've got one strand of commercially-oriented people with this technology and it's about getting access to the technology those entities are developing. Giving access for telling an Indigenous story. Facilitating this is something that I'm keen to talk with our funding bodies about because I think that's the key. What we need is to find a way to provide access to that swiftly changing suite of tools.

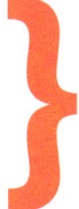

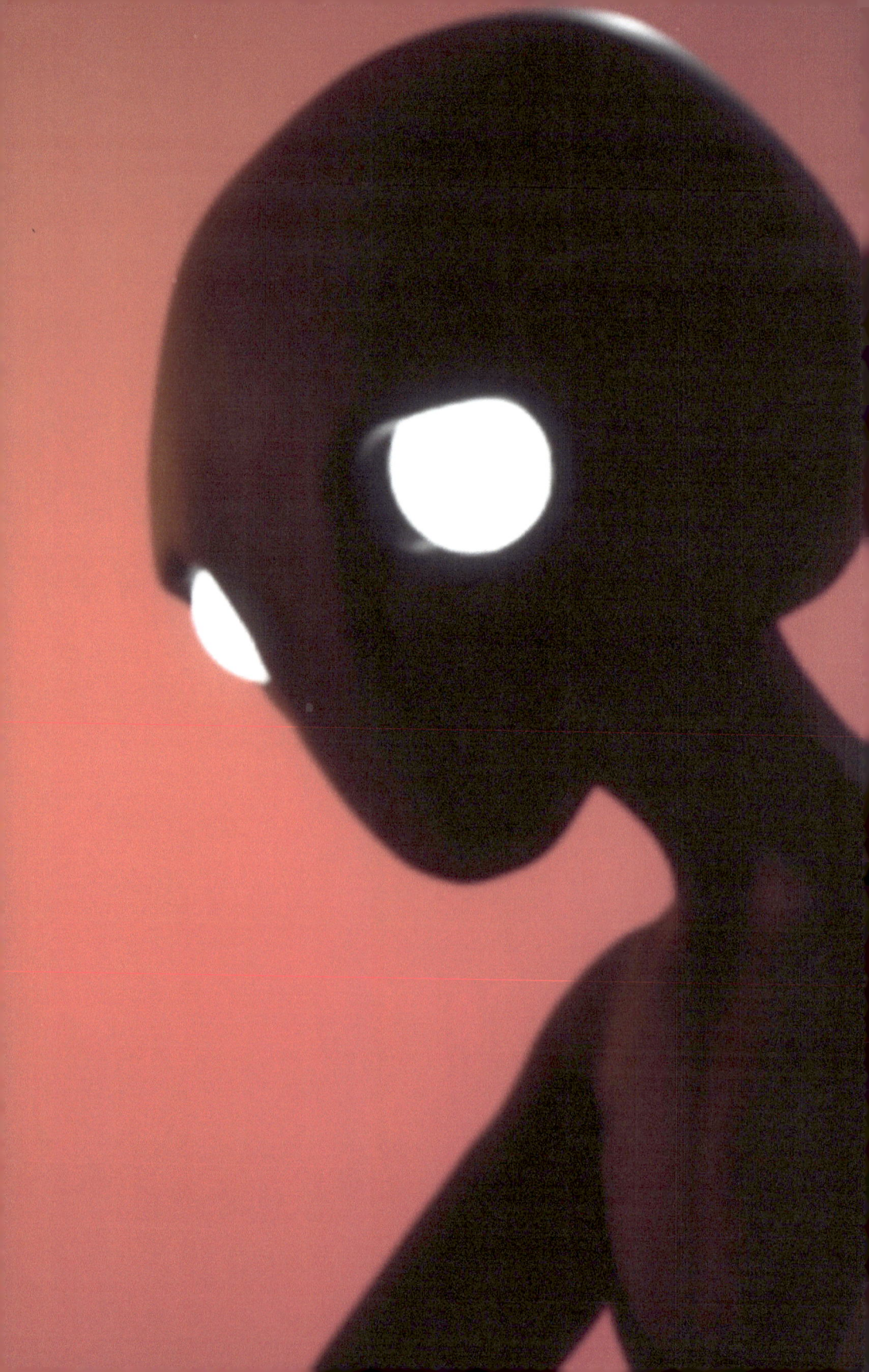

PROJECT BIRRONGGAI
FRENETIC STUDIOS
(VIRTUAL REALITY)

Project Birronggai is an interactive Virtual Reality storytelling experience that explores a dreamtime narrative unique to each player. Through immersive and engaging narrative, the audience is exposed to Indigenous culture, stories and language. This VR experience is the brainchild of Jeremy Worrall, Joel Davison and Keenan Parker, three young Aboriginal professionals working in the tech industry.

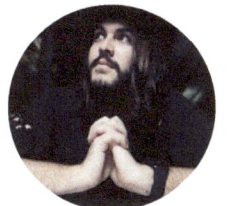 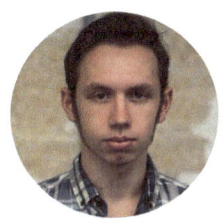 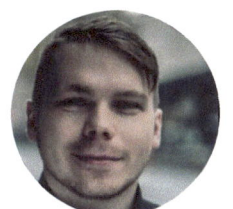

JOEL DAVISON
Operations

KEENAN PARKER
Lead Developer

JEREMY WORRALL
Creative Lead

Joel Davison is a Gadigal and Dunghutti man who is passionate about the revitalisation of indigenous languages. He's currently employed at CBA as a Robotics Analyst. Focusing on the concept of marrying language revitalisation with tech to achieve better outcomes for his community.

Keenan Parker is a Bundjalung and Torres Strait Islander. For the past 10 years he has developed games, websites and apps, working with Indigenous businesses and organisations. His dream is to create games and experiences using immersive technologies like VR, to better express the concepts behind them and to let the player see a world through a different set of eyes.

Jeremy Worrall is a Ngarabal man and a proud member of the Kamilaroi nations, from Emmaville, Armidale. He has a passion for the arts, and specialises in utilising his culture and background to create a bridge into the digital space. His dream is to help bring our culture into the digital art space and show the world the beauty and wisdom of his peoples.

INTERVIEW

{

Angie Abdilla: So I just wanted to start with a personal introduction to yourselves and an outline of what Frenetic Studios is and what your roles are in the project.

Joel Davison: I'm Joel Davison - Gadigal, Eora. My 'day to day' is as a robotics analyst at Commonwealth Bank, however, I'm also heavily involved in the language revitalization of my people's language, the Gadigal language. And that brings me into contact with all kinds of interesting projects, like the one that we're working on at Frenetic Studios.

Keenan Parker: I'm Keenan Parker. I am Bundjalung, and Torres Strait and I currently work as a web and app developer at Ngakkan Nyaagu [NGNY] and I'm the lead developer for the project, so the programming side of things.

Jeremy Worrall: My name's Jeremy Worrall. I come from the Gamilaroi nation up in Emmaville. I work for Cox Inall Ridgeway at the moment, and also work for Ngakkan Nyaagu as a graphic designer and an animator. Mostly just doing Indigenous art and campaigns like that. I am the, I suppose you call it, the creative lead. I do all the modeling and texturing, and visual sides of things.

JD: Frenetic Studios is our passion project. It's our chance to just do what we love to do and work with each other to make that happen. I am on the business side of things, so I'm essentially just managing operational risk and making sure that everything

is provided for Jeremy and Keenan to work their magic on this one. And also voice my opinion where maybe it isn't wanted half the time.

All: *(laughing)*

Josh Harle: So it sounds like you all come from different professional positions and working on outside projects. So Frenetic Studios is just specific to this project, or you've done other projects that have been your own creative drive out of Frenetic Studios with that?

JW: Definitely, just the first project for us as a team. Obviously, we've worked together and Ngakkan Nyaagu, which is at least how I came to know JD and Keenan. But yeah, this is the first major project we've done together outside of work.

AA: Can you describe *Project Birronggai*, the features within the virtual space, and what the players are doing within this world?

JD: 'Birronggai', in my language, means, in a basic translation to English, belonging to the stars. So the project of the stars, or project belonging to the stars. And the virtual space is essentially a story told through a semi-randomized collection of small scenes that the player participates in. And each of these scenes will expose the player to an element of the Dreamtime, or living in pre-colonial Australia. Each will be accompanied by narration that will impart either some knowledge of the Dreamtime stories that we've

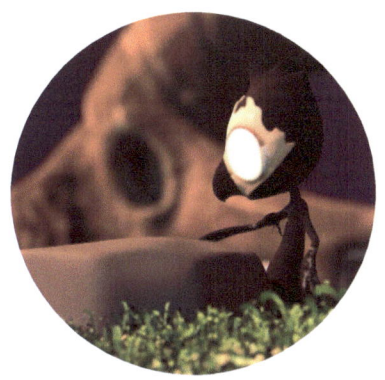

grown up with, or our history, or our languages. Hopefully, if we do it well, all at once. And as the player journeys, it becomes more and more influenced by the Dreaming. And when the player walks away, they will have their own story that was told throughout. It'll be different to the next person's who goes through the experience.

JH: So the randomization means that you're creating a new story from the different components where these different components of the story come in and mix in different ways, and therefore, each person will have a completely new reading of the mix that they get from it.

JD: Yeah, absolutely. This kind of gameplay was heavily inspired by Game Set which Keenan, Jeremy, and I enjoy. When we were kicking around ideas, we were thinking maybe more of a *Rogue*-like [a randomly generated dungeon game], and that's where the random element came in. I think the random element really stuck. This idea of each player coming away with their own story really stuck when we consider the individualistic nature

of our people pre-colonization. This idea that no one person's journey is the same is something that really appealed to us.

AA: I'm intrigued by that, Joel, because at the same time also, an Aboriginal kinship system is very much collective in its organisation. So how do you navigate that when thinking about the way in which your players are going to move through the VR experience?

JD: Yeah, absolutely. I think for me, my knowledge of the kinship system isn't as strong as my knowledge of other parts of our culture. In particular, the totemic system. The ways that we constructed these systems, the totemic system, the kinship system, and how those interrelate, are really strong mechanically. They were very clearly designed with each of these mechanics in place to play their certain parts. And that makes a lot of sense to me when you're thinking of ways to create a balanced story for each individual player. For example, totemic system, you might have a family totem, an individual totem, you have a scale, a feather, a plant. And each of these that inform who you are or you're going to be, or the kind of things that you're going to do, and there will be very few people who have the same combination of totems. But they give you a way to relate to other people. So I would say that we took more inspiration from the totemic system, and my understanding of that, than my limited understanding of the kinship system.

AA: Have you considered how that's going to work with the direction of your players and the intended experience?

JD: Yeah, so at the moment, it's fairly limited, what we've planned. It's fairly limited in that we want people to apply their own meaning to the collection of things that they've experienced. And have that be a way to differentiate that from each other and connect to each other. So we mostly leave that up to play, but that might not be enough for what we want to do because you might have someone who comes in alone and experiences it, and leaves thinking that they've experienced the same thing as everyone else, for example.

But one thing that I think Keenan can talk about more than me because I'm not gonna be as hands-on in terms of the design of the mechanics or the development of the mechanics. But we want to be very strong mechanically. Any mechanics that we put into the game and experience to hold their own and be compelling on their own. But we also don't want them to be barriers to entry. We don't want young people or elderly people, or less able people to not be able to enjoy our experience be of certain mechanics that we put in the game. So we are very conscious of the mechanics that we want to put in the game that essentially tells these stories. And that's something that's going to come later on in development after we've already achieved what we want to achieve from telling the story.

Do you have any thoughts on that, Keenan?

KP: Yeah, definitely. I think definitely the accessibility and having these mechanics interacting with each scene, not be a barrier to our guests completing the scene and moving on between them. Instead, just letting the player experience each scene, even how they choose to, is a big part of it.

JH: Do you have any examples of what type of interactive mechanics these would be?

JD: There's one that I love that Jeremy came up with that I definitely wanna make in the game. It's not a part of my Lore, so I haven't grown up with this story, but Jeremy, do you remember that conversation we had about that particular game around the creatures that would come at the player, and you essentially have to look away when you need to look away and look back to something in their tracks.

JW: Yeah. I'm in the same position though, because it comes from another mob [tribal group], so it's all up in the air. We'd have to obviously consult with Elders on it, but I suppose the general idea of it is, there is a spiritual entity. Essentially, they are these vampiric spirits, if you like, that will sit up in fig trees and wait for travellers to rest under them.

And what they do is they drop down onto the traveller and they have these little suction cups where they will suck the blood out of travellers. Not so much to kill them, but more to feast on them and keep them tied, so they can keep them there consistently and eventually drain them of life. So whilst that's very dark, we had the idea to turn it into a scenario of almost red light, green light. I suppose you call it the gimmick, but the way to get past the spirit based on Lore is if you're pretending you're dead, if you're playing dead, then they won't bother with you, because obviously if you're dead, then you have no life to offer them.

So the idea for the player, in our first-person perspective you can imagine it, is you'll be sitting under a tree, or you'll find yourself in a place where there are a lot of fig trees. And on your journey, you're prompted to rest by Wugan, the character that's guiding you. You'll rest and you'll notice a bit of rustling in the trees. And essentially, without going on too much about it, you encounter this being and Wugan advises you of what it is, gives you the rundown of the Lore and advises you the only way to get past it is to act like you're dead, but at the same time, you have to get away from the fig tree.

So, the first-person player would essentially be looking up at this vampire as it stares at you maliciously, you would play dead, and keep your body as still as possible. And as you look up at the fig tree, you would see him looking at you. And then he'd lose interest or maybe look at something else, and that's your chance to move. You just wanna drag yourself forward

away from the fig trees as fast as possible whilst watching him, but stop the second he looks at you again. Yeah, I suppose that's one example that we're having a lot of fun with and trying to figure out innovative ways to incorporate that into a game mechanic.

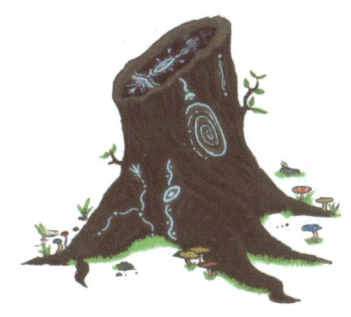

JD: Something that we really wanted to talk about is how we research and now, create history, and how we consult with other mobs, and their stories. From a business perspective, we consider anyone who's Lore or language we're involving. We consider our stakeholders if they're a knowledge holder of that Lore or of that language. We have to answer to them just as crucially as we do to anyone who's provided funding or technology, or mentorship. That's our responsibility to them. If, at the end of the day, mobs who have this as part of their Lore aren't comfortable with us sharing this, or aren't comfortable with how we've portrayed the spirits, or what they do, or what they look

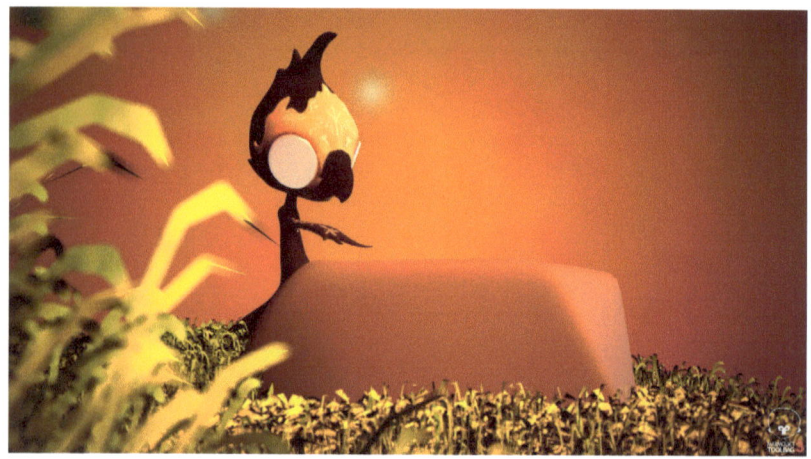

like, then we're not going to be releasing that to the public until they are comfortable with that.

AA: So does that mean, Joel, the culmination of an Australian Aboriginal Lore because you're incorporating a variety of different Aboriginal languages, customs and Dreaming?

JD: Yeah. So this actually ties into our distribution plan. We are planning to distribute this through installations and museums, and galleries and schools, mostly because people don't have access to the thousands of dollars of technology required to run these kinds of experiences. We want it to have some sense of longevity. We also wanna tell our story, but we also wanna allow other people to tell their stories through this framework that we're building.

So the plan at the moment is for this initial release of this project, is going to be our stories and the Gadigal language specifically. And I don't think we're gonna go too far outside of the stories that are a part of our upbringing and our mobs. But post-release, we want to collaborate with other mobs and let them tell their stories through our platform.

JH: Do you want to talk about the two figures that you interact with in the environment?

JW: Yeah, these two characters, one of them is obviously traditionally cemented in the Lore, Biame. So he varies, actually, and you can find him in any of the cultures around the area. But essentially, Biame is what they call the Sky God, or the All Father, and he's featured in the game. He's pretty much the first character you encounter in the game.

TECHNOLOGY AS CULTURAL PRACTICE

So basically, you enter this game, what we call the Dreamtime. It's this surrealist environment that mimics Country or the land. But it has stylistic, surreal attributes to it, as well. You're in this vast landscape, and you're prompted to move forward. It's very foggy, very dark, mysterious. There this cinematic spectacle of these two bright eyes that pop off in an inescapably fast direction upwards, like a very tall being's eyes come out of the fog. Then there's this spectacular sound from this giant moving over a mountain and comes down to you with his long arms, and lifts up the very earth that you're standing on.

So he digs his hands into the earth and lifts it up as you would with soil in the palm of both your hands. As he brings up the landscape with you, and he brings you to his level in the clouds, the fog clears and Biame is revealed, as he is talking to you in language. I suppose he'd introduce himself, in a sense, and impart this journey or quest onto you. And the character Wugan, he is this little creature, he's based off a bird native to my mob in the area, and he is the personification of Biame. So I should clarify, Wugan is a name that we decided upon. JD, I think the direct translation is 'large bird', or am I mistaken?

KP: I think it was crow specifically.

JD: Yeah, it's a type of crow, I'm fairly sure.

JW: Yeah, and so this Wugan character is formed next to you as you're experiencing this entity and this play zone that he's created just by lifting the earth from the ground. Wugan, basically is Biame, but he is, I would just say the personification. He is a champion if you like. So, Wugan will stay with you throughout the entire experience, translating or telling you the wishes of Biame, guiding you through the game and all the different characters you meet. So I suppose, yeah, that's the two characters. Biame is traditionally in Lore, and Wugan has been created by us as a way of guiding the player throughout the experience.

AA: Indigenous and non-Indigenous audiences are going to receive the experience differently, so who is the intended audience?

JD: We wanna be able to say that this experience is for everyone. We hope as much of our family and our mob come to see it, they love it, and they're proud, and we hope we can take it around to show some mobs in Australia and see their reaction; learn from them about how close it might be or how different it might be from their Lore, or their understanding, or their experiences. It may be a good conversation starter about language as well. But I also think white Australia would have an extremely different experience. For all of us, these are stories that we've grown up with, or on our periphery, and we're all familiar with it.

It will be a fresh take on something that we're all very used to. But for many white Australians, it might be their first genuine interaction with Dreamtime stories, and experiences.

They might come away from that being like, "Whoa." I hope getting a real sense of how different from Eurocentric storytelling Dreamtime stories are. And then, of course, in almost everything that I do surrounding culture heritage and language, there is an insatiable appetite from tourists for genuine Indigenous made content and stories. So we really wanna hit all those marks and I don't think that's gonna be too difficult to do. Well, not impossible, anyway.

KP: I definitely think also it lends itself towards slightly younger audiences, even ones that are gonna be teenage.

JW: Yeah. I think Keenan's right in that a younger audience would be drawn to it. I think our goal is to fit everybody in. Obviously, there's a limit to who we can put the VR headset on, but we would like to create the stories that are accessible by all age groups, and perhaps, all walks of life. Indigenous Dreamtime learning, it's amazing, but it's fundamentally important for our mob, and just other folks to see it and realize the majesty of it. So, I suppose in the development process, in terms from an artistic perspective, you're working with these Dreamtime stories. A lot of them are quite dark in the sense that they are warnings. I think with the art style that we're using, it should be accessible to most, it shouldn't scare off too many people.

AA: How is *Birronggai* going to enable or leverage the revitalization of Aboriginal languages?

JD: I'm glad you ask this question because there's a very direct answer to it. And that is that one crucial part of revitalizing our language is finding uses for it. We live in a capitalist, liberal society where things need to prove their worth by providing some kind of value to people's lives. Usually, monetary value. But also, artistic value, or the ability to improve someone's life, or outlook, or even let them unwind so that they're more effective in different parts of their lives. So a big part of my job in language revitalization isn't just researching the language, isn't just teaching the language, isn't just using the language myself, but it's also finding uses for the language, not only for myself but for others.

And not only just for my language but for other Indigenous languages as well. Because what I found is that the revitalization of one of our languages sets off a chain reaction. It's intimately tied with the revitalization of the rest of our languages because the same conditions required to really revitalize one language are the same conditions to revitalize another. So if you can create those conditions for one language, you can do so for all the others. So hopefully, me finding a use for my language in this and having that be a use that others can find for their language in this format, some of those conditions where they're revitalizing their languages, that will flow on to the market and vice versa.

AA: Is there a strategy for the incorporation of various different language groups within this one VR experience and game?

JD: Yeah, at the moment the model that we're after, because of lack of imagination, is the standard video game post-launch DLC model. Where you have the base game, which is the project that we want. And then we will create essentially packs of content in collaboration with other mobs, and release it, essentially, siloed as its own thing with some generic content from the initial release mixed in with it. But now that you've mentioned it, there can be some interesting possibilities with how we can have those interplay. And that's something I've been thinking about semi-recently with some more revitalization work that's been coming up.

JH: We could ask the question of why you chose to use VR rather than any other approach. So as a first-person game, for example, what do you think the VR brings to the experience?

JD: I think there's plenty of answers to that one. That's easy.

JW: Yeah. We all flew to the idea of it unanimously. Naturally, it was weird. Joel has a VR headset that was lent to him by a friend that we had in the office. So he showed us what the HTC Vive was like. I'm sure you'll understand when I say that it's nothing like you have ever experienced before. It's this bizarre feeling of immersion that you don't necessarily would get from a computer screen or a TV screen. I think testing this on my Mum, I noticed that generally, she's very against video games, but the one time I showed

her, she was almost sold on the idea of video games entirely. That spoke to me in a way personally, that you can create a video game and show it to all walks of life. It's so intuitively easy for them to pick up and understand because of how immersive it is.

I feel that would definitely benefit a project or a subject matter like this because it's the best platform to do it the most justice. The Dreamtime, it's so deeply rooted in our cultural thinking the only way to truly portray it, at least the best we can currently, is through the VR space I would say. I'm not sure if you guys would agree with that, Joel and Keenan?

JD: I would say the caveat to the intuitiveness of VR is if it's well designed.

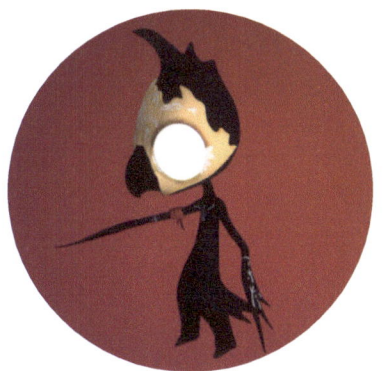

JW: Definitely, yeah. There's a lot of shockers out there, so we're obviously gonna learn from that, hopefully. And I'm confident that we can bring an experience that is intuitive and well received, hopefully.

AA: Was there an immediate conclusion that this experience that you're creating in VR is being led by a gamification model as opposed to, say, for example, a pure immersion experience?

JD: I would say that we definitely approach it from a gamification lens. But with how accessible we want it to be, there's definitely room to argue that it's more of an experience. But I think, at that point, it's more semantics than anything. We would like game mechanics, but we're not gonna get anyone for not being able to do certain things. And I just wanna add on to the emotion side. For me, personally, I think the ability to immerse people into the mythical, to really sell them on the idea that I believed when I was camping when I was younger. That there's a hairy man just over the ridge, watching us while we're sitting around the fire.

That's something that's incredible. That's something I want other people to feel. Yeah, so the emotional element is very important to the kind of story you wanna tell about the Dreamtime to other people.

KP: Yeah, I think me and Joel actually talked about this early on in the conception of the scheme. But I definitely brought up that we need to make sure that we're doing things like game mechanics, to really gauge someone's progression through our experience with it. That more of the experience was towards those art games. Josh mentioned Dear Esther earlier, which I was a big fan of. We

take more of an expression from those while having the game's mechanics as an additional side part to the game in a way.

JH: Are there any game mechanics that you think would be beyond just being an extra bit to what's going on in the story, ones which are absolutely fundamental to the story? And these could just be moving through the space in a certain way rather than some complicated form of interaction. So rather than things that might add to the story that are not necessary for progression, because you don't want to lock people out if they're not interacting, for example, an interactive element where you don't have to worry too much about the level of abilities, but that is fundamental to the way that the story is being told or what is happening in the story.

JD: I would say that the only necessary interactive element is the ability to hear or read the narration and look around and experience it. That's really the key to it. We don't have any other solid interactive mechanics locked in place, I would say. Is that correct, Jeremy?

JW: Yeah, I mean there's obviously a few that we talked about. There is traditional spearfishing. Interactions with the vampire spirit, as we said, but there isn't anything fundamentally that would stop the progression of someone that could physically not do it. Obviously, it's challenging if you'd like it to be, but if you're there for the experience overall, to learn the languages, and to experience the different stories, then I would say, and you guys can correct me here, that it would be as accessible as possible.

KP: Yeah, definitely. And I think another thing that you could see as the core mechanics in the experience is we've talked about walking around and pointing out things that are narrated in language. So they could tell you about the language for a river and we're gonna walk over to the river and show you that that's what it's relating to.

AA: And how is the story within *Birronggai* being revealed and experienced within the game?

JW: I think the way we're trying to initiate a play zone that is created, like a hub world, if you like. That's basically what Biame is holding. It's the middle point in between stories, or progressions. The best way to describe it is that there is this stone which will change. The stone will feature loose sand or loose dirt. Wugan will stay there and whilst you're in the hub world, creating patterns or trails of art in different forms as a place called 'rituals'.

Those rituals will open. It's like a level selector. So it will open you up to a certain experience depending on what he draws in the sand and what you select. You will then be transported into that ritual or that story in which you will experience. Then upon completion of the story you'll be taken back to the hub world and the process starts again.

AA: So is it narrated by the two main characters, Biame and Wugan?

JD: Yeah, so essentially each of the stories, we haven't really nailed down the terminology that we're using, so we should probably steer away from that. But we look into the stories that the player's gonna play through. It's essentially just a collection of scenes, and each of the scenes is an environment with narration and potentially an interactive element. They are semi-randomized in their order and some you may or may not see. So it's not a clearly defined story in terms of the hero's journey, where there's always be a beginning, a challenge, and end. It'll be more like a disjointed trek across Country with all the notable experiences along the way being experienced by the player.

JD: And yeah, shared through narration or subtitle.

AA: Coming from a film background I'm interested in VR because of its potential to break out of that traditional three-act structure: beginning, middle, and end. There's a huge opportunity to explore Aboriginal circular story-telling, which is far more akin to a 360 environment than traditional storytelling structures that are squeezed to fit inside the box of TV or rectangle of cinema because it's linear.

JD: Definitely.

AA: So have you thought about the story and the traditional ways that story and Lore is passed down? As

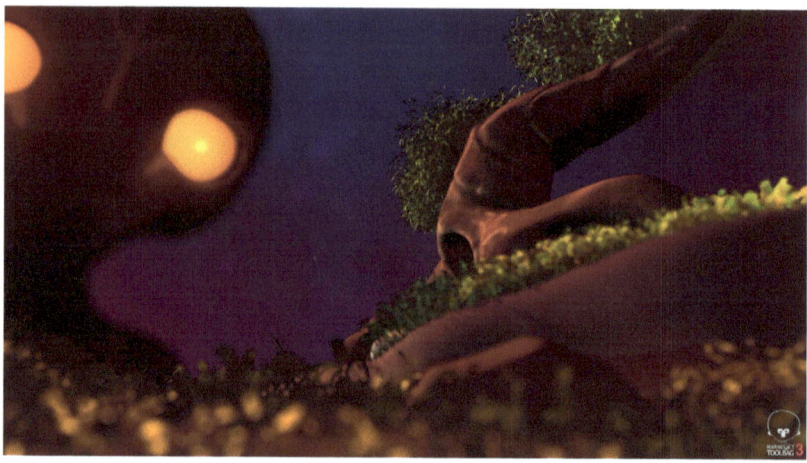

with the traditional transmission of Aboriginal knowledge being through the act of singing that same song over and over through repetition and time that the knowledge is revealed, the deeper code to that knowledge. Is that something you imagine you're able to tap into for your player's experience?

JD: I don't think that's something that we've explicitly discussed, but I do know it's something implicit in each of our experiences with game design and each of our experiences with Dreamtime stories. So we haven't said explicitly, "Hey, the repetition and replayability play into the story that we wanna tell." It's more of the story that we want to tell will naturally create this kind of experience. And that's because Dreamtime or the Dreaming is strictly nonlinear. It's not something that's 1400 AD, et cetera, happening and now we're here. It's never present, as the past was the future, and the future is now the past.

Just knowing the video games that we enjoy do heavily feature that kind of cyclical gameplay. I think the main inspiration I can cite for that is the *Dark Souls* series, one, two, and three, and *Blood Born*, and *Demon Souls* are very much so these kinds of games you play the first time and it's its own experience. And then you start over again with a new game plus, and new game plus plus, and plus plus plus. It's a completely different experience. You experience all these different things, and uncover all of this that you didn't the first cycle around. Even the Lore in those games is heavily focused around this cyclical storytelling, maintaining the cycle, or breaking the cycle. Yeah, it's a heavy inspiration to all three of us, I can safely say.

Is that correct, Keenan and Jeremy?

JW: Yeah, definitely.

KP: Yeah, I can definitely agree.

JH: In some of the other interviews people are coming more from a creative space without the technical background, and they've had to go and work collaboratively with tech people, find people to work with, and their exposure to technology has come about in more sort of accidental way. Whereas you all have technical skills.

Keenan, with your computer science background, it would be interesting to know how you feel the creative process has manifested through coding as well. And don't worry Jeremy, everyone appreciates the creative process of what you do!

JW: The programming is creative, that's for sure.

KP: Yeah, so for this project, as of yet, we've mostly been learning around the *Unreal* engine process and developing VR using that. I've definitely enjoyed experimenting with creating things in a way that you open up gateways for the designer, like Jeremy, to pop in and change some things on the back end within limitations that you give them. It just seems like there's a lot of collaboration between Jeremy seeing a lot of the same things I do. Working together and actually building out the physical side as well as him. It's not just him shipping models and things like that to me, and then me building everything based on that.

It's a very collaborative process, though we haven't had much experience in that yet with how it will lead us in development.

AA: Do you think that there's been a different approach to learning *Unreal* from an Indigenous standpoint? Do you have alternate development processes that reflect this alternate perspective and understanding that everything is connected and interrelated as one complex system as opposed to a traditional linear development approach?

KP: Yeah, that's definitely an interesting question. I can't say I've really thought about that too much. But yeah, I think that's definitely something to think about moving forward, even just looking how some of those things may have subconsciously affected me. But I can't say that's been a really conscious decision in any way so far.

JD: We haven't really talked about it in these terms because it was most explicit and obvious when we did the exact opposite. When we chopped up the process and divided the labour, and said, "Okay, Jeremy, you're gonna sit over there, and at the end of the day, you are delivering assets to us. And you're not gonna know how they're used, and you're not gonna see how they're implemented until we're in the testing phase where you can see it." When we divided the process up like that and stopped collaborating as closely as tools like the *Unreal* engine let us collaborate, that's when we started having conversations about the nature of the work. So I think it is definitely something that was in our subconscious and that's definitely shaping how we're going to be structuring our processes and our inclination towards tools like the *Unreal* engine.

JW: I agree completely with what JD was saying. And I think, Angie, that question that you posed is a fantastic one and I think it's something that I'll take forward with me throughout the development process. I suppose if I had to think about it now, the collaboration with Keenan and JD, it's very open and very transparent. I would say it's considerate in the sense that with game development especially, you can't separate yourself from the developers as a creative, because then you're just going to be stepping on toes constantly, providing assets that they can't necessarily use, creating bumps along the way. I think as a group, me and Keenan, during the development process will be so closely knit that with the *Unreal* engine specifically, they have a blueprinted engine now implemented that allows creatives to, as Keenan said, get into the back end of it and the front end of it and really see what's going on so that there is a constant communication between dev and creative that maybe once wasn't there.

I may be working alongside him constantly. I will know exactly what he needs and why he needs it, and vice versa. I think that'll create an environment that would just simply prosper even in the learning phase of it.

JH: So you have already talked a little bit about that process of consulting with different stories from different groups, but do you want to talk in general about that process of composing different scenarios, how you got access to them, researched them? And maybe a little more about the consultation presence?

JD: What we do plan to do is whenever we do presentations, appearances, or demos anywhere, we'll always ask if there is anyone who is a knowledge holder in relevant fields who wants to join us along the journey and become a stakeholder of ours to ensure we do things the right way. I think this is gonna be a bit of a learning journey for each of us three to take these stories that we may have grown up with or grown up around, but we don't strictly know enough about it, or the history to create solid content for the experiences. Then, to go back to our own families and learn more thoroughly from them and pursue other resources in the community. I know that we're for sure going to be spending a lot of time in as many universities as we can get our foot in the door at, and speaking to as many Elders who are knowledge holders, and reading from knowledge holder's past, as well.

AA: And why universities?

JD: So I think if we're going to our families, we're going to the community's universities just to present that other side of the spectrum, where you have people who ... Well, we hope we will find people who are very passionate about their study of it and have a different perspective than family and community resources. Students, professors, faculties. Anyone that'll talk to us.

AA: So it's expanding the knowledge, not necessarily about the technical assistance.

JD: Yes, exactly. Although that being said, we're not gonna rule out the possibility of discovering some interesting technical knowledge about storytelling or history and having that shape how we're going to go about the process.

JH: It sounds almost like reclaiming stories. It's certainly the case that there's Indigenous researchers in universities, and academics such as yourself, Angie, who are writing insightful papers and research about the process of storytelling. But at the same time, it sounds like there's an opportunity to reclaim culture, to take back stories from academia. It's outside of most people's accessibility, and then bringing them back into a way you are telling them, according to your decisions and approach to doing it which is also quite exciting.

AA: It sounds like a process of repatriation.

JD: Definitely. It's a very exciting concept to go to a university and find stories that aren't held by my family anymore, and going to my family and community and saying, "Hey, how would you like to see these stories presented in this completely new format." That's something that's just mind-blowing.

JH: The language teaching process of it: has your approach to teaching language come from research or an 'on-the-ground' sort of way for communicating language?

JD: I've been teaching language for a year and a half now. My prior education experience was teaching culture and heritage at the Botanic Gardens, mostly tours, talks, and things of that like. I've just been running so fast, trying to maintain my career, trying to get projects like *Project Birronggai* off the ground, and trying to revitalize the language in each of the ways that I've outlined before, being research, teaching, doing, and finding ways to do, that I haven't found a spare minute to learn how to teach.

JH: So is that something that you're going to put work into? And can you give us the context of why teaching with Duolingo [a language app] for example is not appropriate, or there's a better way of going about it?

JD: Yeah, absolutely. So of course, how to teach it effectively in this medium is something that I'm going to put a lot of work into, because we don't want any of the mechanics that we might develop to detract from the experience, we don't want any of the attempt to educate people on language, or culture, or stories, to detract from the experience either. I think that's just as important as letting bad mechanics through, not letting bad techniques for educating through is just as important. The Duolingo question is a really big one.

I would say, to keep it concise, the two biggest reasons why our language doesn't lend itself well to that format of teaching is, firstly, because those platforms tend to outsource the benefit of that education to the platform holders.

That is to say, if I begin to revitalize the language, and I go back and I teach my family, and I give them a complete package for how to teach the language so that they can contribute to revitalizing language. They can go and have opportunities to engage with the community, and learn, and have more experience, and potentially mature. Also, a very large part of it, is getting paid for doing that. Whereas if we plop that on a resource like Duolingo, we suddenly lose governance over how it's taught. None of those benefits are translated back to our communities. They're instead paying the Duolingo platform holders through advertisements.

The second attribute that doesn't lend our languages to being taught in a platform like Duolingo, I think is that platforms like Duolingo are an effective way of teaching people how to use the language if they have the motivation. That motivation, more often than not, comes from having a very solid use case for the language. But right now, the vast majority of people who would be learning the language would be people who don't traditionally hold the language. There's only so much Gadigal mob out there, that even if 100% of us went on Duolingo and learned Gadigal language, we'd still only make up a

very small portion of the user base. And the rest of the people who would try to learn the language wouldn't have as much motivation as us because they're not gonna say, "I'm gonna learn Gadigal language so I can go visit Sydney," because they can go visit Sydney and speak English.

Whereas if you go to Paris, you almost have to speak French, and similar for every other use-case that a lot of the languages that are on platforms like Duolingo have.

JH: Yeah, my feeling about a lot of those language learning platforms is they don't teach culture at all. If it's for teaching a businessman how to speak another language, it's basically a misogynistic 1950's model of how to pick up a date when you're on a business trip in the bar of your hotel without any cultural context whatsoever. Here's what you say without engaging in any way about the cultural use of that language. They seem to believe all you need to do is substitute one word in one language for another word in another language to have the same effect in the experience in a different place.

JD: I 100% agree.

JH: What do you feel are your responsibilities as storytellers?

JW: That's a question that I think we've asked ourselves a few times. Maybe not exactly like that, but as a collective, we've talked about it a fair bit. JD, do you have anything, to begin with or should I talk from the creative perspective first, or would you like to...

JD: Just to say that we feel a lot of responsibility.

JW: Yeah. Definitely that. I suppose from the idea of actually visually displaying these stories in a VR medium. Obviously, it goes without saying that that's not how they were originally intended. And there's gonna have to be liberties, or creative liberties, taken with those stories in order to display them visually. For example, the model that I created for Biame is based off the traditional cave paintings found in the Biame cave, as well as some other illustrations that I've collected, and from what I've just been told based on the description. The way he's come out is as traditionally accurate as I could keep it. But it's obviously not to the T, so that's definitely something that I'm worried about in terms of conveying these stories visually. I don't want to put my own idea, or spin, or the team has their own ideas and creative elements into it. I don't want to, for a lack of a better word, butcher it. So that comes with a lot of responsibility that Joel, and Keenan, and I will all help each other with based on community engagement and the primary sources that we get those stories from.

AA: Are their any cultural protocols that are built into the design of the experience?

JW: I suppose touching off the creative again, all the body paintings that you see on Biame, they don't feature in the initial conception of him, at least from my sources. So they were additions on my behalf that I put in. If you look at them, they are all taught to me to have meaning. So for example, the main, he has a mark on his forehead, which is a mark of a bird, essentially. A general interpretation of it would be a bird track. This obviously holds meaning with what he is and what he represents as a Sky God, along with the markings running on his chest going down his arm. The pathways, without going into full detail, one might be circles, would represent a place of meeting, place of home, gathering. The pathways represent just that, pathways, rivers, and so forth. There are symbols for people gathering, as well. The C shaped or the U shaped symbols. So yeah, I suppose to answer the question, there are pretty heavy cultural protocols in the design of the experience that is in no way hindering me. They are only benefiting me because the beauty of Indigenous design is that all these symbols have multiple meanings and multiple feelings to them, which you

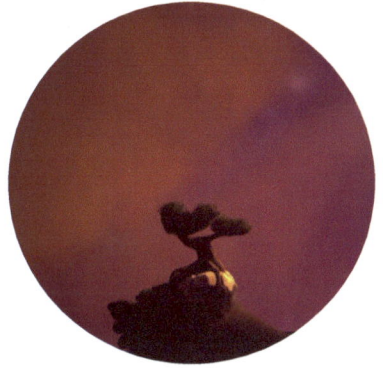

can compile together in such a way to tell a multitude of stories, which I find remarkable and beautiful. So I find that that is definitely going to feature heavily in the game because we're lucky enough to be able to work with content such as that.

JH: Do you have any advice to people who are starting out, and any other projects that you can recommend having a look at, or which were inspiring or informed your project? ...We're also interested in how everyone experienced VR for the first time.

JD: We actually more or less all tried VR, or at least dived into VR in the exact same way. My friend had a headset, and I borrowed it off him, took it into work and we all tried it.

KP: My initial experience was actually at this place called Coderfactory which is where I went through a short course on the web film stuff I do. But that's where we held the first Indigitek meetings that I went to. One of the people from there, had a Vive [VR Headset] set up in the office and

they just let people hang out and play. That was my first time with a Vive or any sort of non-mobile phone VR headset. I think most of it was just going through the Steam VR lab and maybe a bit of VR Accounting. So part of that, Joel actually brought his ... I can't remember exactly which mobile one it was.

KP: I think it might be the Samsung Gear.

JD: Yeah, Gear S6.

KP: We actually played a couple of things on that, one of which was a horror game. I think just going into that and just feeling, even though the graphics were low quality because it was new in its mobile VR, just the atmosphere and the scale of having to look up at something and just how different that sort of a motion makes a game was a big part of what really inspired me to push more towards learning VR as opposed to other game development.

JD: As for how we decided to do this project, we worked together at

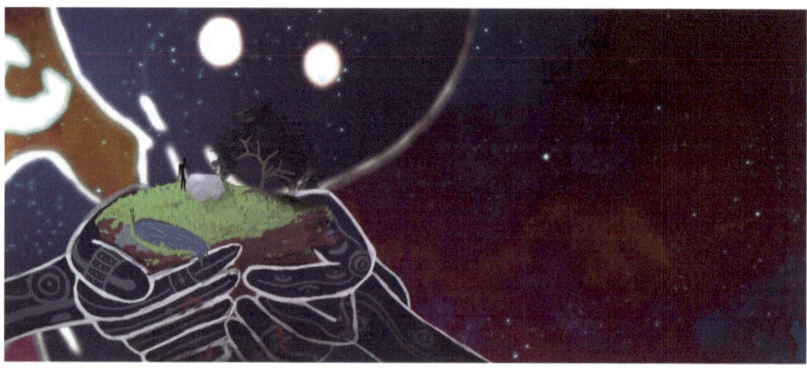

NGNY. And I guess these two missed me enough after I left. No, it's just something that I think has been a dream of all of ours and we've had the requisite experience to do it between the three of us. So it was just natural.

JW: Definitely.

JH: So for developing this experience, did you feel it was necessary to get up to this point where you're all skilled up and you've got the experience before engaging in this project rather than jumping on it and learning from scratch.

JD: I think it's empowered us to be more audacious about the specifics of the experience, and really at an artistic level, this is the messaging that we wanna put across. Without having to worry about if we are capable to do so - we're instead asking, "Alright, what is the best way to do so?"

AA: Yeah, and there's another layer to the process when you need to explain the nuances of cultural protocols when working with non-Indigenous developers.

JD: Yeah, exactly. 100%.

JH: And also, they might not be very good. If you want to do something special, you know what your capabilities are, you have an idea that you can spend a few late nights figuring out how to do it. Whereas if you're working with an external thing, they just do what they want to do, what they're comfortable with.

JD: I actually heard that complaint. In my current role, I sit in between the business and consultants who are developers, and I heard the exact complaint today. It seems more like they're developing what they want to develop rather than what we need them to develop. It would be a shame to have a project like this fall prey to that kind of practice.

JW: Definitely.

AA: What are your thoughts on the current state of Indigenous digital media? Are there any other projects by practitioners that you'd like to mention, or advice about starting out in the medium?

JD: Yeah, I think I speak for all of us when I say that a large part of what drives us on this project is that this is, not to discount what anyone else out there is doing, but Indigenous digital media is not at the point where we want it. I hope that after we do this, and after we keep doing projects similar to this, potentially, that there are still people ten years from now who will say the same and keep pushing it forward. Yeah, I really don't wanna discount what anyone else is doing out there, but we want to see Indigenous digital media thrive because we feel like it's worth it. We feel like there's so much that is out there to be told and so many interesting and talented people to tell all of these interesting things that are there to be told, and so many interesting mediums for all of these interesting people to tell all of these interesting stories! And interesting

TECHNOLOGY AS CULTURAL PRACTICE

lessons to share. It's just a shame that it's not as vibrant and thriving as we would like it to be. So we would like to contribute to that. I think it would be irresponsible for us to share comments about getting started in the video gaming development.

JW: Follow your dreams.

KP: I think as far as other projects, there's actually this guy Rhett Loban from UNSW who's making a game very heavily influenced by astrology based VR experience as well. I think that's definitely another one to check out.

JH: All of our different interviews reference each other. That seems like a good sign!

JW: As it should be. Everything should be interconnected. We've all gotta help each other out.

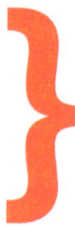

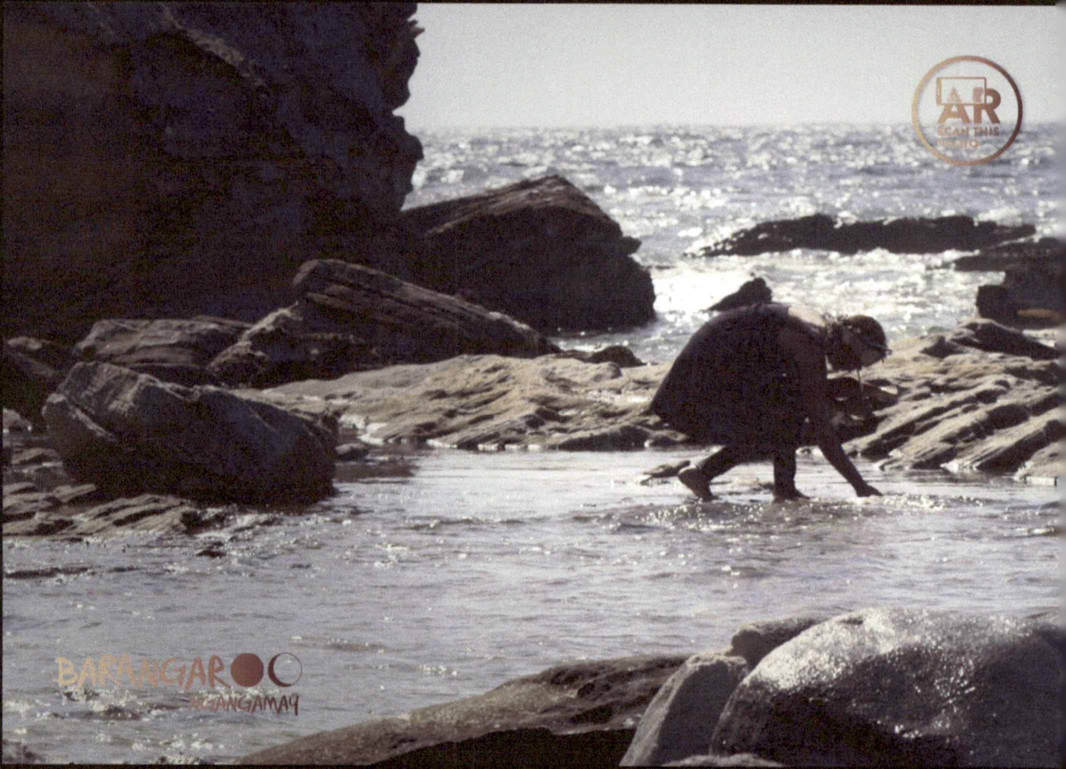

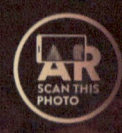

BARANGAROC
NGANGAMAY

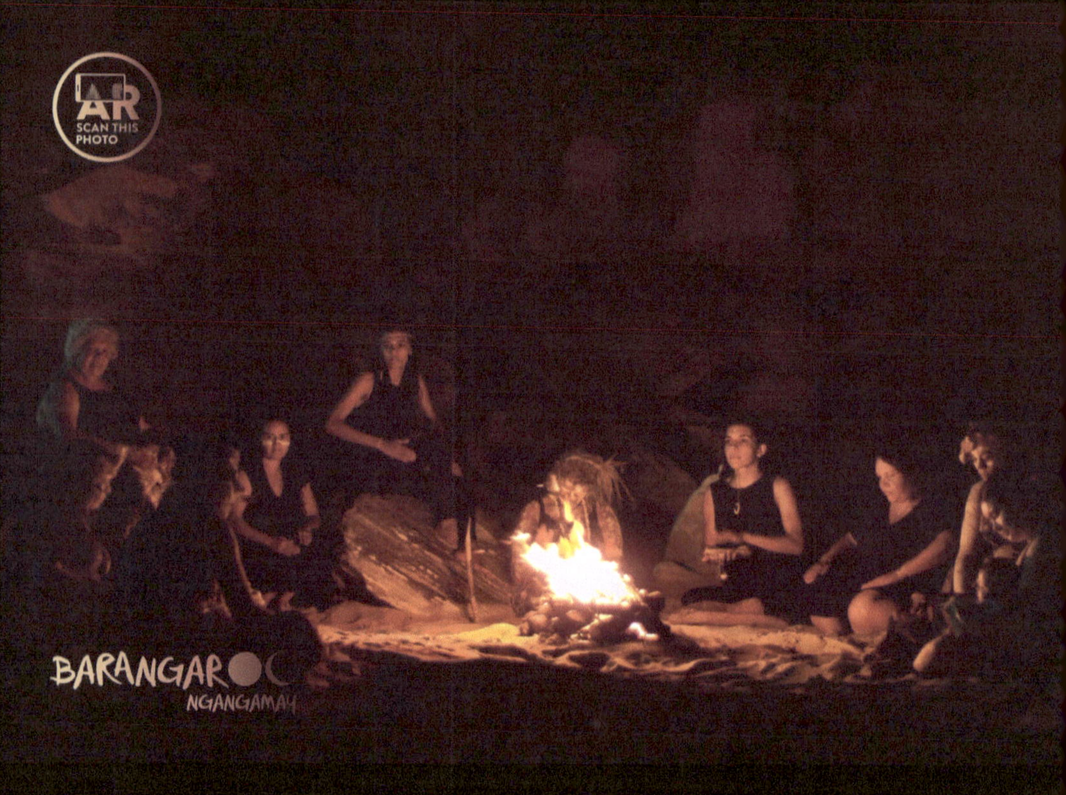

BARANGAROO NGANGAMAY
GENEVIEVE GRIEVES & AMANDA JANE REYNOLDS
(AUGMENTED REALITY)

The images facing can be used with the Barangaroo Ngangamay app.

The name Barangaroo has become common parlance among Sydneysiders and visitors who regularly enjoy the spectacular Barangaroo Reserve and the new retail and dining precinct. But what of the proud Cammeraygal woman Barangaroo, after whom this culturally-significant area is named?

This strong and influential warrior woman provided the inspiration for Barangaroo's first Artistic Associates, renowned Aboriginal multi-media artists and curators Amanda Jane Reynolds and Genevieve Grieves.

Reynolds and Grieves were appointed as the inaugural Artistic Associates by the Barangaroo Delivery Authority to collaborate on a multi-disciplinary program that celebrates the history and culture of the local area and its peoples.

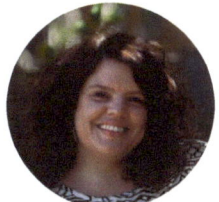
GENEVIEVE GRIEVES
Artist/ Curator

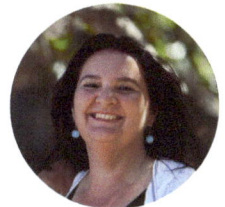
AMANDA JANE REYNOLDS
Artist/ Curator

Genevieve Grieves belongs to the Worimi nation of the NSW mid-north coast. She wears various hats including film-maker, educator, curator and oral historian. In 2010 she wrote and directed the award-winning documentary Lani's Story for SBS about a young Aboriginal woman's journey from victim to survivor; while her engaging five-channel video Picturing the Old People was exhibited in Australia and abroad and is held in collections with the Art Gallery of NSW and the Queensland Gallery of Modern Art. Her video installation Remember, commemorating the lives lost in the horrific 1816 Appin massacre, forms part of With Secrecy and Despatch, an exhibition which opened at the Campbelltown Arts Centre in April 2016.

Amanda Jane Reynolds carries family heritage from Australia and other parts of the world, including Aboriginal (Karingai), African (US), Silesian and many British and Irish convicts. Reynolds is a respected curator, cultural consultant and editor who runs the organisation Stella Stories, specialising in collaborations with communities, museums, galleries and heritage sites to produce stories, exhibitions, multimedia exhibitions and cultural programs. She has worked with the Australian Museum, National Museum of Australia and the National Film and Sound Archive, among many others.

INTERVIEW

TECHNOLOGY AS CULTURAL PRACTICE

Josh Harle: Thanks, Amanda, for talking to us about yours and Genevieve's *Barangaroo Ngangamay* work. One reason I find *Barangaroo Ngangamay* so interesting is that having spent time researching virtual reality and augmented reality, it's clear AR games like Pokemon Go have this problematic power dynamic, where one corporation somewhere in the world can just suddenly dictate the meaning of all spaces without having consulted or visited or anything. They just press a button to launch and suddenly all of these meanings are retrofitted and applied to the world.

In general, I think augmented reality projects have got problematic politics, with the exception of projects like yours where it's about reclaiming space and bringing a history to the fore, that is located at that site that might not be visible to the outside observer. You can bring that back and illustrate for people who are visiting the site.

Can you give just a general background to yourself and Genevieve, and the project?

Amanda Jane Reynolds: Genevieve Grieves is a Worimi woman and she's a very talented curator, artist, filmmaker and oral historian. She's a very big-hearted, beautiful woman whose really committed to community and community empowerment and collaboration. Gen and I worked together on First Peoples at Bunjilaka. I'm Amanda Jane Reynolds, I'm Guringai and I also have convicts, so

I'm both invader and invaded, right there in Sydney, on the other side of the harbour. I'm a curator, a possum cloak maker and I work in multimedia.

I actually felt a strong calling from Barangaroo to come to this project many months before the artistic associate's opportunity was advertised. I had talked to Genevieve about some of the things that were coming up and this desire to continue and honour the women's business. Of course, there were many other women all feeling the same thing, wanting to do more, to come together. Then the artistic associate came up, so it was one of those things that resonated at the right time. We felt a strong calling as did other women we connected with that we wanted to do something for the Ancestor, Barangaroo, not necessarily a biography, because that wasn't what the message was, but an honouring of the strength of Aboriginal women through the generations.

Our collaboration is a pledge and a commitment to continue women's business and to continue coming together and to continue holding that place and that space right there in Sydney into the future. To step up and to do our jobs, and these are our jobs, to ensure that future generations will have that presence. We're also very conscious that most people know Barangaroo for the new development and the suburb now, so there's a duty for us to ensure that Barangaroo is remembered as a woman, a very powerful, inspiring, strong, beautiful woman who was right there at the

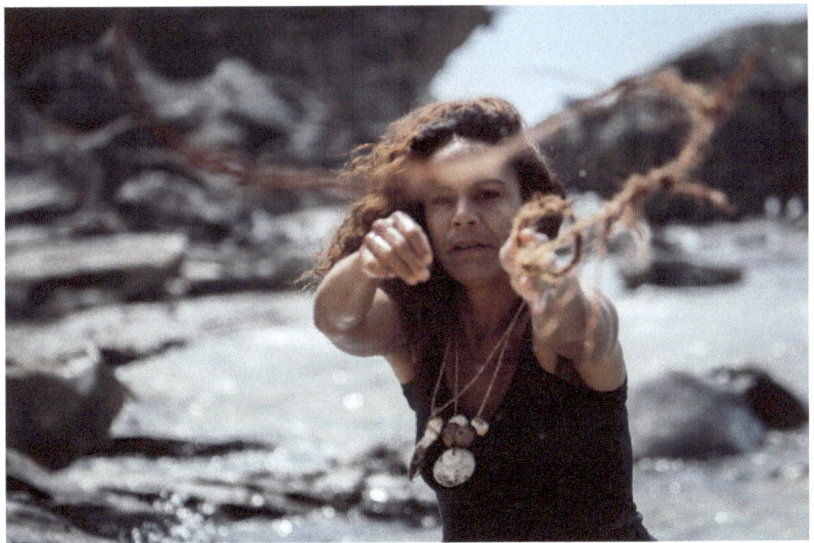

time of the invasion of Sydney and the changes she went through in her life were extensive and traumatic.

She lost her children, she lost her husband, she was there when Arthur Phillip came, saw the beginning of what would become the rolling frontier, the colonisation and the invasion that later spread across of the whole of Australia as we know.

The work *Barangaroo Ngangamay* is an honoring of Old Lady Barangaroo, who lived during the time of the invasion of Sydney. It's a coming together of women and men from Sydney clans and further beyond to make a promise that our culture will continue and that we will keep our stories and our cultures alive in the Sydney region. It's an invitation to visitors from Sydney, from Australia and from the world to come down

to the reserve at Barangaroo and to listen and to learn and to experience the beauty of culture embedded in Country or in a site. No matter the season or the weather you can go on your own personal journey in your own personal connection through the use of an app that you can download for free from the app store and go on an adventure around the site.

We wanted to do healing and we wanted to bring the idea of a cultural journey and that story exists in place, not just story, but people and particularly because we're in Sydney where there is the assumption of there's no Aboriginal people, if there are they're all a certain way, so we really wanted to use the technology to bring people back on site. Real-life people. The capacity of what the Augmented Reality medium can do is as wild as our imagination. But for us this work was also an opportunity for us to do community projects, this project happened to be seeded as a women's project through the inspiration of Barangaroo herself. We are both curators at heart in that sense of we love holding a space to bring in lots of collaborators, lots of other people through our practice and projects that have a healing and strengthening component and a journey as well.

We did a call out to women, to traditional owners and then Aboriginal women living in Sydney as well and running a series of workshops that were behind the scenes and didn't have to have a public outcome, where women could sit and learn from elders if they wanted to or share stories and just gain something through the experience that always didn't have to have the pressure of a public outcome. That we could just use some of our money to come together to strengthen culture, because again that sense of continuing women's business was our number one priority throughout the project.

The culture camp and workshops were good because many people wanted to come and talk about things and share and learn but didn't necessarily want to be involved in the project and others did so we think that's really important especially when often funding is given towards tourism outcomes and to Aboriginal people creating content to be consumed by the general public. Sometimes shifting the balance of oh well, let's get our foundations and let's invest in our communities

for that healthy culture within our own spaces first so we can then share with the broader public. I think these things are important no matter whether you're writing a book, an exhibition or technology. Technology doesn't change the importance of the commitment to community and to Country and to those strengthening cultural practices. It's one of those things that I think is about a process of working that's critical that goes across many mediums.

JH: That was a fantastic background to the project. For those who haven't used it, could you describe what someone's experience is if they go out onto the reserve at Barangaroo and uses the app?

AMJ: *Barangaroo Ngangamay* is a site-specific work utilising AR technology through a free app. Visitors can then interact with the artwork through their own personal devices and their own real life journey walking around the site enables them to either search for or stumble across hotspots where short films, songs, photos or story can be accessed. Sometimes those hotspots are marked in the real world by a rock engraving created by senior men and linked through a symbol on the app. Sometimes the hotspots are marked in the real world by elements of Country that are less obviously 'signposted' such as the rise and fall of sun or moon at certain times of the year and linked through a photo or symbol on the app.

Whether the visitor consciously recognizes it or whether it's in some subconscious experience; they are immersed in the journey, in the story, in Country and their own walking on Country at this site is multi-layered through the technology, the weather and the path they choose to follow and which content they access. As you move around the site a different story belongs there, you can't see all the stories at all the places, you can't take the phone home and watch the films as they are only accessed at geolocations so you have to be there.

In one sense it's based on one of the foundations of how our culture works. The Creation Ancestors did all of their businesses and then they sat down in Country at certain places and that's where they belonged. Sometimes that's the only place you can sing these songs or hear these songs. There's a way of knowing and understanding Country that is so desperately needed by modern Australia, because if people understood more (and there's a lot of people interested and wanting to learn) about our land management practices, our respect for mother Earth, all of those things. We felt like we were giving strength to ourselves and our collaborators too by coming together and making a promise to that old lady Barangaroo. We're going to do our job, look after this and we're going to keep trying to teach and show people these values and help them understand that. There's an underlying purpose that we want people to understand Country better.

JH: It's great to be able to talk about how augmented reality responds to this idea that here's a lack of

sensitivity or there's something that's going on that if you're not prepared to be audience to you'll miss.

It's more than just using AR as an engaging technology. You are using this technology in a way that resonates, a metaphor for a way of seeing in a site as well. A haunting or presence there that some people will be aware of and some people you have to switch on and get an idea of what's going on there.

The other thing that I found really interesting was that your efforts weren't focussed just around an augmented reality product where you just sit in a lab and make 3D objects and tag where they appear in the site. You were documenting contemporary practice of the site that was at least as important as the experience of the videos in augmented reality, after the fact. The focus on going out to Barangaroo and practicing the site for the project is really exciting.

In some way, it's a different medium to film, for example, but it's one where you can have a very visceral experience, when you go to a certain location and you see those videos, for example, it's very much about being there and things going on and these echoes of things that have happened in that location which is very different from any other way of doing it for sure.

The technology is often used as a novelty, for projecting some sort of fantasy-future, like a spaceship or whatever, into the space. And for your use of Augmented Reality,

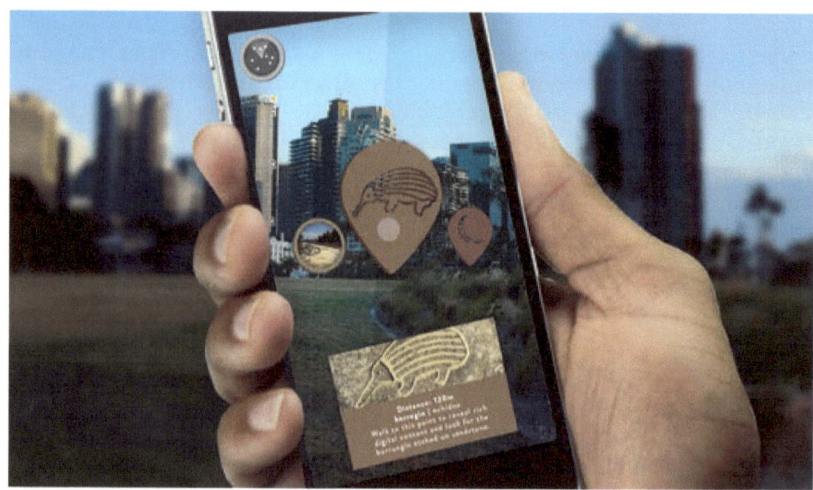

the importance was to represent a presence.

AMJ: That's strong on your decolonizing theme.

JH: Yes.

AMJ: Decolonizing technology. The fact that we're in the center of Sydney, but also anywhere in Australia has had some form of the erasure and destruction of country through colonisation, I mean that was also the motivating reason. Culture continues because of the old and because of the new, because of the previous generations, because of the past generations living in the Creation era. Time collapses. And so on one level we're developing the app. And on the other hand we asked some of the senior men, would they lead the men's business and engrave the rock onsite. The greater Sydney basin is one of the biggest rock art galleries

in the world, it's a major site and a lot has been erased through the building of the city.

And so it was a chance for the men, and they speak very emotionally and are so deeply proud of what it meant to be able to come and put those engravings on the site. And that would continue into the future alongside the technology, I mean everyone was crying. We are all crying all the time because of what that would mean. And it's like technology alone didn't have that solution. It was all of these things together. The concept of the past and the future coming together in the present; the technology (whether stone tools or digital tools) being put to use to continue culture, strengthen people and Country, and reveal a layer of the presence of Aboriginal people.

The Old People like the Old Lady Barangaroo knew Country on a level that we don't know because of invasion and colonisation and language that has been lost. But we know it and experience connection on another level, at this moment in time and after colonization. Both Genevieve and I and our collaborators who shared culture and came together through this project, were inspired to do the best we could and to keep learning through collaborative, creative and cultural practice.

We wanted to honour the old people's deep knowledge and connection of seasons, the environment and astronomy. And to renew some of our neighbouring clan and songline connections in the Greater Sydney Basin - the artwork and cultural experience has generous and inspiring contributions from so many people including Gadigal, Bidjigal, Garigal, Dharug, Yuin, Guringai - the coming together of people connected through the old songlines and trade-routes and family relations. It's not that often that custodians get the opportunity to come together to work on a Public Art project in their region and so this work is also a pledge that there is always a place for Aboriginal people in the city. It's still Aboriginal Country, the Reserve is on Gadigal clan land and the words of the Aboriginal human rights activists who have fought for community and for Country since the invasion 'always has, always will be Aboriginal land', although not explicitly stated, resonates through the presence of the artwork. In one humble way it is contributing to presence instead of absence.

Visitors to the site may or may not engage, some people don't know about it, some people walk past everything, some people want experience, some people will go out of their way to learn. And that's how we are right now in modern Australia.

JH: I mean the idea of having the represented things in the augmented reality it's like, if you're with the right set of eyes and the right sort of way of seeing, you wouldn't need any of those cues. You just see all of these things that wouldn't be apparent to me, for example, looking around and seeing things. But that different way of perceiving and knowing, for example, that this is when the wattle is going to bloom and this is when the fish are going to be there. There's a few questions that are really interesting that have come up from that. I suppose one of them is how would you think about the use of technology as a continuation of indigenous cultural practice?

AMJ: Absolutely, I think it's key in the 21st century. And I think I get so excited by all these young people like in Digitec, and all the young generation. Aboriginal people are massive adapters of mobile phones, of technology, of all of those things, of keeping connected, keeping a community, creating new spaces. I don't know if you saw Black Comedy last week where they had a skit of a dance group called the "Wigglymuyu Dancers" painted up and doing a dance for tourists on how their mob communicate and the song goes "Facebook, Instagram, snapchat, tinder - no reception, no reception dance". It was very funny take-off skit but true on how important communication technology platforms are for community.

I've had the great privilege as has Genevieve in our lives, through museum work, of sitting down with Elders, particularly from the southeast, but from all over Australia as well, and hearing about some of the challenges around cultural continuity and intergenerational transfer of knowledge. And so many Elders we've heard say, "We've got to get to them on their phones." That's what they're spending all their time on. And we need to get onto their phones, how can we get onto their phones? So, I mean the background of this project was also a thing of, "well, they'll be on their phones." And part of that 'how to get on their phones', it's not just because kids are spending so much time in a digital world or kids that we know, Aboriginal kids are really big adapters of this technology. So many Elders see the importance of exploring new mediums.

When you are breathing you're living, when we take our last breath we're no longer living. And when we're speaking, we're hearing the vibration of our voice. So even more than seeing, the hearing and the voice is so important. And so that's one reason song people and songlines are so strong and so important. And they do go over time and they go over distance and they have important points along a journey. And this modern technology that we can take with us and access content at different points is in my

experience, far closer to the old ways of knowing country than a book or a film. Not that I don't love those mediums, I love those mediums, they are so important and we need to have all of these mediums. But it gives you a chance to understand, you can only get this story here at this place, by this person, not by everyone. And it's in a different context if someone tells it to you somewhere else far away. But it's connecting the links between people and Country.

So it's actually a way to strengthen the knowledge system rather than to sit in a room, dislocated from a season or a star or. So the old ways of knowing can be strengthened if you only release content at certain places or at certain times. And this medium, or if you're with somebody, a certain person, there's a whole lot of potential in this medium for actually strengthening our knowledge systems and our ways of knowing and learning in stages and at different sites. That sometimes the pressures of the modern world are taking us away from those ways of knowing. Does that make sense?

JH: Yeah, absolutely. It's very different from sitting down and talking. This idea of sort of global, non-contextualised knowledge, like everything is sort of horizontal access with things like Wikipedia and Google where they just consider everything completely equivalent.

I still find it amazing and kind of creepy that I can sit down and use google maps and zoom into places where I've lived before and what it looked like the last time the Google van drove by to look at it. The idea that we have all knowledge completely accessible universally without any context, is definitely a very sort of 'Google' way of thinking about things.

And Google's had heaps of problems with that way of thinking about the world coming up against, for example, their belief that they can drive those cars around and capture everywhere and then show it to everyone.

In Germany there's rights to privacy that have come out, in Japan their cameras were higher than the average height of people's building fences, so they had to lower them because there was an expectation of privacy. Many problems, especially around mapping, coming out of Google and just them not realizing that they don't own all knowledge and they can't just provide it always.

AMJ: I know an Aboriginal community who took on Google and got their little community erased from the map. The detail of, "alright now you're on this or that community." Erased. And they took them on really early on I think, they were like, "these streets were around, they're not."

Anyway, they got it all removed. Like obviously the outline of the coast and everything is still on there. But their little street maps, you can't look up their street names or get the thing on there, on this one little place.

JH: Well, hopefully Google is learning. I don't know if it's completely at

odds with their approach to thinking about the world, but hopefully they're learning some lessons in there.

One thing that connects into your idea of creating access to different types of knowledge, is the fact that the sited experience of spaces with Augmented Reality is fundamentally in sympathy with the sort of stories that you're telling and the way that knowledge has been shared.

One question that I have is about that choice between watching the women fishing in the midst of the women's business and the men's business. What was the thinking around the presentation of either of those two? Did you have to think about cultural protocols, like sensitivity around representing women's business and men's business in the augmented reality system?

AMJ: Yeah. When I talked about those issues, about the capacity for the future of technology, we haven't necessarily utilized all of them to their full capacity in this particular work.

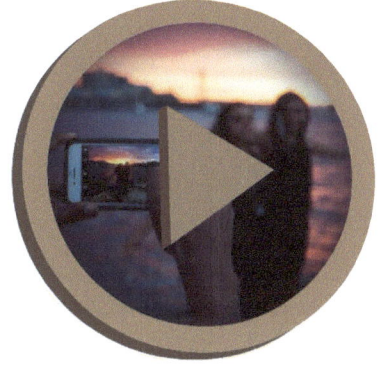

So our main emphasis on this was around the women's contemporary song cycle and our invitation to the men, honours the strength of men's business. Their project was incredibly significant, particularly the rock engraving aspect and that we wanted to give glimpses into the Elders creating that.

So the one thing we did talk about with everyone is, especially the Elders, is if they pass away, can we continue? Because we do have the capacity to remove content from a medium like this and they all wanted it, everyone wants it ongoing as long as it's there. So we did have that conversation and people very strongly felt, "oh, we want this now to stay." So that was one of the cultural issues that may have come up or may have a different context in different communities. Otherwise we already knew we were making the work for the public, so our choices all along the way were very much, while we've got all these priorities about what we're doing, we're sharing this work with the public. So we only created content that was shareable. Am I getting somewhere with the sort of question you're asking?

JH: Absolutely. And also it sounds like what you were doing in the initial stages, the thing that you finally rolled into the augmented reality experience was entirely in the context of having conversations with everyone involved about how it will be presented.

I think that's really interesting, to be able to give people an understanding of what comes along with the

technology and to be able to give informed consent for example, and think through. For me, especially from a technical background thinking through, because pretty much a whole swathe of the technology already has western cultural assumptions built into it. So when you have to think about cultural concerns that also illuminate some of the western concerns, if you know what I mean.

That Google approach to thinking about knowledge isn't neutral, it's a particular cultural way of thinking about knowledge. So just that thing of like, "okay, we had to think about the allowance of removing people. If it was necessary."

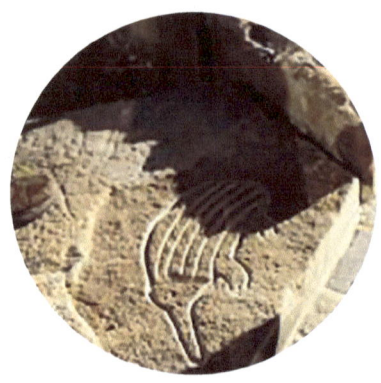

Can you speak a bit about the intended audience and how different audiences might come to the experience?

AMJ: Well Gen and I share this sort of approach to what we do, if we say the word community, we say it with the understanding that community's incredibly diverse. Everything we do, we always go, "it's going to work for community." Which again, there's complexity in saying that, because community is so diverse and so different. But with each project you define who the stakeholders are. So, that's really important to remember that Aboriginal and Torres Strait Islander people are an audience. And not just an audience as a consumer, but a student that could learn culture from their Elders through this artwork. There is an importance to intergenerational experiences. It doesn't always have to be learning, it can be just connection or cultural experiences.

We are also always trying to show that there's a lot of diversity in our community. There's old diversity, in terms of, the cultural diversity of different clans of the Sydney region or the Southwest, or the North Coast or the West. Some people are possum people, some people are mullet people. That sort of traditional diversity, and there is contemporary diversity. Some of us, like me, have multiple nationalities from around the world as well. Some have lighter skin or have darker skin, some speak a certain way or have different accents, there's a huge, incredible contemporary diversity of lived experience on top of that as well.

It's just the sense of trying to be true to the beauty of the ages and the diversity, and the way we are in the modern world. The fourth scene featuring the young Madden women, we filmed that onsite with the city and their background, Gadigal right

there, city, country. Our sound editor actually had the idea of bringing in some sirens and sounds into the soundtrack, which works so beautifully, because visually we could see all of the city lights there.

We're so used to only seeing a certain type of person on our consumption of TV, or a certain age or valuing women of a certain way they look, or see, or feel. Through this work we celebrate the different ages of women, it's something that underpins who's in it and what we're doing. It's something, I think that some people, other older women might really respond, from other cultures might see their grandmother there, or go, "hey, I know that, I know grandmothers because I've got my grandma. I am a grandmother and I've got grandchildren. I've got a grandmother." I think having that presence of the different generations, which is so fundamental that people can recognize it in their own cultures as well. It's a way in for some people to connect.

JH: That's definitely not just through representation in digital media art. At least when you start looking at what is mass produced and mass distributed, things like games. It has such a narrow area of representation that's getting slowly better, there are lots of projects that are doing good things to widen that set of what type of people are represented in them. Your project has also managed to contribute to the wider representation of diverse women in that sort of medium, which is fantastic as well.

AMJ: The other thing is, we don't really have spoken language in this. We only have song language and we have no translations. In the museum world, because of things I believe in around accessibility issues, you often have captions for hearing impaired as well as the label and sub-title translations into English. But as an art work, you don't have that pressure. It doesn't really matter if people don't know the exact words because your spirit feels this little film clip. You can just experience the song cycle for the voice and the sound, and the imagery and the beauty and the poetry.

We were creating little poetic moments because I really feel, and I felt this my whole life, too much experiencing of culture is done in a very didactic way. And to me that's a very western approach as well. And there are benefits to that, I'm all for loving learning through all of the different ways, but we can't lose the fact that our song cycle structures and our old gatherings, corroboree, coming together are so potent in the creative arts as communication - body paint, that art that's on your body, that's on the surface, that links to that constellation that's there right now. That's the song. A lot of people say we have no writing. And through this project I said, "we do have writing, these are symbols, these mean something, if you know what they mean. You just don't know the multi layers that they mean."

So, to me that was another interesting thing, that some people might be frightened that our audience wouldn't understand, because there was no caption underneath. But no one actually complained about that at all.

JH: The caption at the bottom is like what anthropology has done. The idea that you can sum up, make sense according to the Western academic way of thinking and often get it completely wrong as well. It implies that there's an easy translation from one thing to the other and that it's something you dismissively make sense of with a little caption at the bottom saying this is x, y, z.

AMJ: Absolutely, and you're actually taking away the capacity of people to learn, to start to look at all these other kinds of processing information. When people keep looking at the caption, often people don't learn. The argument I often make is, do people learn football and all the rules of football because there's a little thing down on the bottom of the screen? Does a caption describe if that man was tackled? Or do they watch it enough, and listen to it enough, observing and learning so that they slowly start to understand the rules. Some people might have played, so they learned it through that. But millions of people watch football - have they read the referees conduct rules or whatever? No, they haven't. They've watched enough and listened enough and seen this to understand the thing through stitching together the elements and repeat experiences. In some ways it's the same principle, to put this didactic label on it is taking away audiences' capacity to take the time to learn through many senses.

JH: It's like saying that this thing in itself doesn't have agency to communicate to you. The thing that you should be trusting is the institution's caption to communicate the knowledge, which is a little bit of a violent turn to the original, to go, "okay, we're mediating your experience to the original one because we're the gatekeeper to what your understanding of this thing is."

AMJ: Yeah, to make it clear, we didn't have this problem at all with this work. It was at another institution, that experience. So sorry, just in case when this gets communicated, that didn't come up for this work!

JH: I think we're just about getting close to the end, do you want to talk about future projects that you're working on?

AMJ: Future projects that we've got ideas for and future projects that are funded are two different things. There is one project we really want to do using this medium, but in terms of what that is, we're sort of keeping that a bit quiet, because we want to get funding for it, but it relates to exploring 3D a little bit more with figures and scenes in Augmented Reality; a women in a canoe on the harbor.

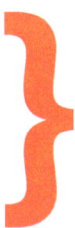

Full Credits and Acknowledgements for Barangaroo Ngang̱amay are available at: https://www.barangaroo.com/the-project/arts-and-public-program/artistic-associates/barangaroo-ngangamay/production-credits/

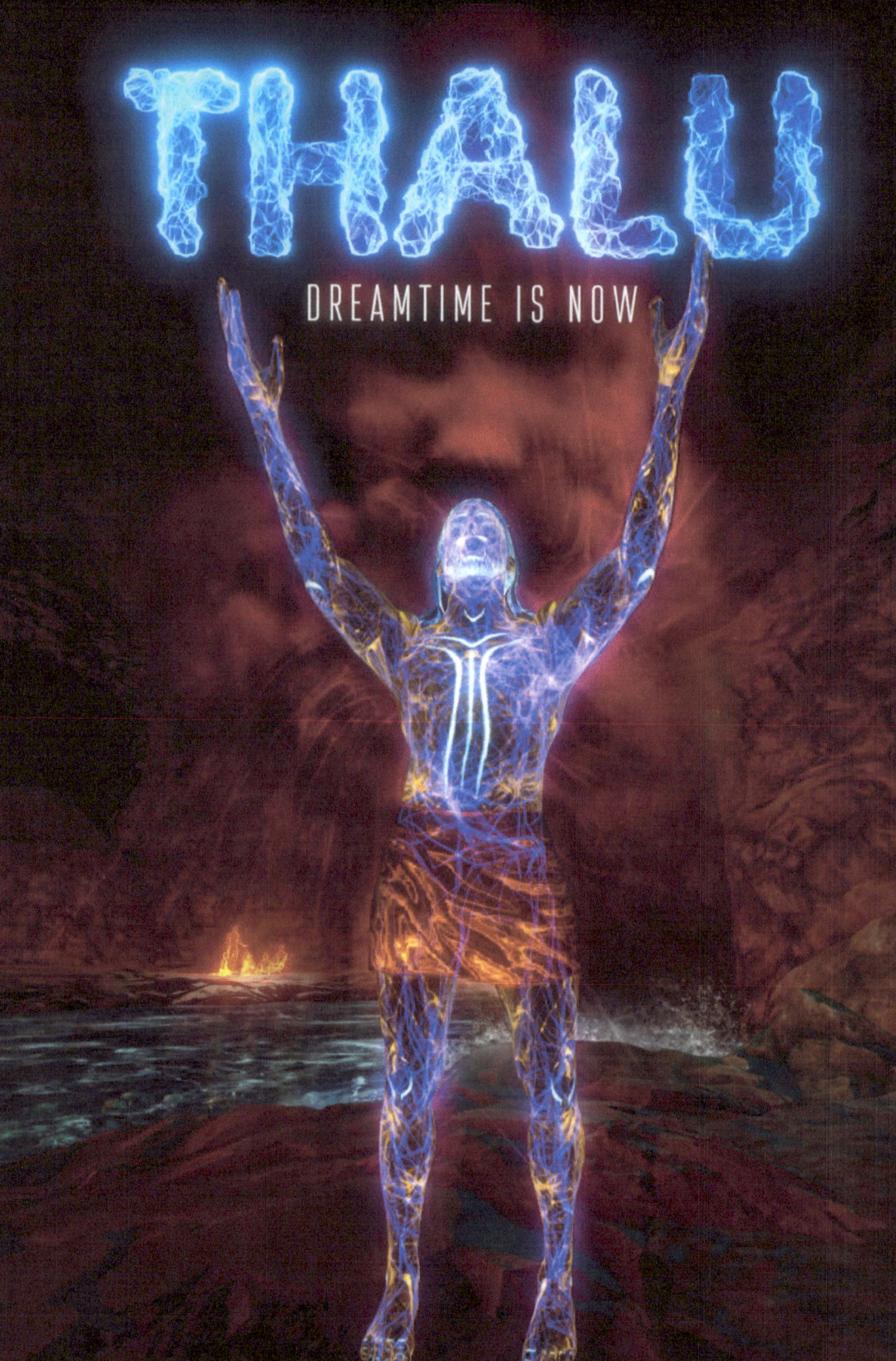

THALU
TYSON MOWARIN
(VIRTUAL REALITY)

The world of *Thalu* is brought to life through Virtual Reality (VR), in otherworldly surroundings guided by the concept art of cult favourite and graphic artist, Stuart Campbell. The VR experience is a dazzling series of linked worlds filled with fantastical, high contrast, neon-lit Australian landscapes and wildlife.

'Thalu' in the Ngarluma language means 'totem'. However, the English word cannot fully describe the layers of meaning that "thalu" conveys to the Ngarluma people. The 'thalu' in Mowarin's virtual reality experience is a spiritual doorway that connects two realms and transports the participant into the Spirit World, where they will meet Jirri Jirri, their guide. Jirri Jirri will show audiences the spirits of the elements, land, flora and fauna, and teach them about how these spirits and environments are connected to humankind.

Launching on the HTC Vive, *Thalu: The Buried VR* is a uniquely Indigenous Australian experience that showcases the powerful storytelling of the Ngarluma people of Western Australia.

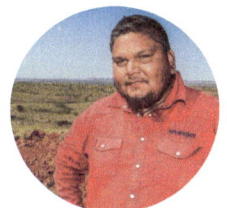

TYSON MOWARIN
Creator / Cross-media storyteller

A Ngarluma man, **Tyson Mowarin** is an experienced filmmaker, writer, producer, director, photographer, cinematographer and owner of Weerianna Street Media. Mowarin's other projects include the *Welcome to Country* iPhone app, an extensively researched information portal and archive of Welcome to Country videos and messages.

INTERVIEW

Josh Harle: Can you tell us about Thalu?

Tyson Mowarin: 'Thalu' is a term we Ngarluma use for certain sites on the Country. It could also be a friend, a little messenger, like a little messenger bird or something. A little spirit that hangs around with an individual. Or It could be a friend. If I've got a best friend that follows me everywhere, people might call him a Thalu. But for the VR project, Thalu refers to certain 'increase sites' on the Country. To compare it to something, it's like when a farmer goes to church and prays for rain. Supposedly God hears his prayers and sends rain to him. A Thalu site on Country is very much the same. We've got rain sites as well. Rainmaking sites where people go out and perform a certain ceremony at a certain site. They can work that site and they can ask for rain as well, and the spirit of the land will send rain to them. There's all sorts of Thalu sites. There's good ones and there's bad ones and there's flora ones and there's fauna ones.

JH: We've been through *Thalu* and seen the different sites. There are icons which indicate which ones there are, and I think there's one for fish, one with a kangaroo symbol. Another one with the whirlwind and the rain coming through. The rain one?

TM: That's the elements one. You can go out on Country and you can summon the elements. Rain and fire, lightning, all that sort of stuff.

JH: Can you describe what the player experiences when they go into it?

TM: For the fish Thalu site, obviously we're not allowed to put the traditional use or the traditional ceremony in the game, what you do there is the player goes down into the water and his little Thalu, which is the Jilly-Jilly bird, turns into human form. Then he hands you the boomerang and there's a certain way that you hold those boomerangs near the water and then that summons the fish up the waterfall. The fish spirits are going up the waterfall, up into the waterholes on the country. Same for the flora and the fauna one. Once you're doing the actions with the boomerangs, which you take with you, you will see their spirits arising from them and going up into the real world.

For the experience, we start by talking about the creation. Then the world comes out of the ocean. Then you're taken down into the Burrup, or the Pilbara - it's all the same sort of landscape - surrounded by all the ancient rock that holds on the petroglyphs, the rock art. Each of the virtual spaces is typical Pilbara landscapes. The spinifex. The specific or the iconic Pilbara rock landscapes, some of these rocks are unlike anywhere in the world, or anywhere in Australia at least. Each of those worlds is what I call the cultural or the spiritual warehouse, where the spirits of all those elements, flora and fauna, live. That's where they come from because even when the farmer goes to church and asks for rain, the rain has to come from somewhere. In my eyes,

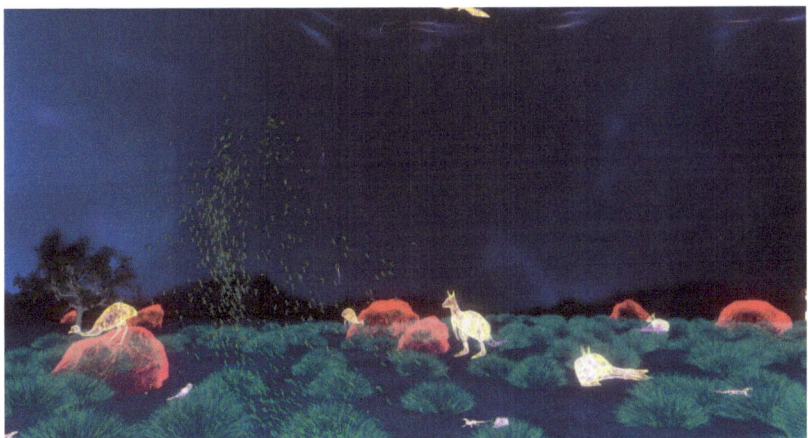

and my theory, according to me it has to come from somewhere.

As you know, Aboriginal culture is very spiritual. I'm saying that those worlds that you're experiencing, they are spirit worlds. That's why the flora and fauna and the elements look spiritual, are all there just waiting for their spirits to come to the real world.

Angie Abdilla: Can you explain what the player is doing within these worlds?

TM: Right at the start, the fish, where the waterfall is, is about learning how to use the fish Thalu, the fish site. He's got a person that's got to learn that they have to use the boomerang to summon the spirit of the fish to go up to the real world. Same in the elements world. You're gathering the power of the elements. Then you're shooting them into the Willy Willy, which takes it to the real world and unleashes it up there. Same with the flora and fauna. Once you're working the boomerangs in different ways, you're summoning the spirits of that

flora and fauna. You'll see the spirits rise up often. They'll leave and up into the real world.

For me, the most important element of the experiences is teaching people about the spirit world, having people see it as a living, breathing thing. It's current. Even it's similar to the Dreamtime, where people talk about the Dreamtime as something passed. Like today is a dream time for me. Today is my Dreamtime. It's the same, the spirit world exists today, not only in the past.

JH: We noticed that being introduced in the intro as well, where you talk about the contemporary landscape, with mining coming into the Pilbara and into the Burrup, and in some of the narrative, where the voice is talking about the setup and the environment, you're talking about how this sort of thing has been forgotten or there's not an understanding of it and these sites are being destroyed, but they're still deeply important. With that in mind, who is the intended audience for this experience?

TM: I always say, everybody. Then it'd probably be younger kids, maybe teenagers, mainly because it's best to teach people when they're young. When you get to my age, you've got a little bit of an understanding about the surroundings they live in.

JH: Talking specifically about damage from the mining industry that's going on in the Pilbara, would you say that there's a focus on making people, for example, in Western Australia where there are all these mining operations going on, a little bit more aware of some of the consequences of this, like the potential damage to these sites and things like that?

TM: Yeah. It's all relevant to all the work I do, and things I say, and in my films as well. My 'Connection to Country' film that I made recently is a documentary that talks about WA's Heritage Act and how the government is trying to amend it. They wanted to do massive approvals for mining and resource companies to destroy sites. Now with the change of government, they're actually reviewing the whole Heritage Act from the community, across the state. A bonus that the new Indigenous Affairs Minister is a blackfella himself. Yeah. *Thalu* is about teaching people about conservation of their heritage as well, because, in my film, my 'Connection to Country' film, we talk about Thalu sites for the plain kangaroo, that they stay on the country here. That one is potentially being destroyed. It might not be a coincidence that you go out to that certain part of the country and you don't see many plain kangaroos.

In our way of thinking, the Elders' way of thinking, the Thalu there is being destroyed so we've lost an opportunity to increase the kangaroo population in that area.

Then, on the other hand, there's another site there for the bush gum, and he's still intact. Right across our Country, in late September, early October. Where that Thalu site is, they start earlier. They come earlier to Country. It starts in that area and then it spreads out. Every year is exactly the same. If that site is destroyed like it's partially destroyed now, it will probably mess the seasons up. If it's destroyed forever, who knows what will happen to those plants. Then they're gone.

JH: Can you talk more about changes to the Heritage Act? I remember they changed definitions to a very Western idea of the sacred site, based on churches.

TM: You know what they actually did was they deregistered nearly 4,000 sites right across WA without consultation with Aboriginal people, because they brought in a classification to say that a sacred site has to have a regular religious activity attached to it. If you compare that, like always compare the Aboriginal Heritage Act to the Build Act in Australia, even manmade churches don't have regular religious activities. Still, they are listed in heritage listings, and they are protected, and you can buy and get the money to restore them and maintain them. Whereas, an Aboriginal Heritage site you can't. For

Indigenous sites, they deregistered them all and they didn't tell anybody. It was only found out by accident.

AA: It strikes me as a potentially precarious position to be in, because of course there are cultural protocols with who information is shared, in particular within a virtual environment, as opposed to on Country.

TM: Teaching young people about heritage sites when they're young - the audience is broad. Hopefully. When I build these things up I don't really think of the audience until it's built. Heritage should be protected by everybody. That's something non-Aboriginal people have to stop and think about as well, even when things happen like NAIDOC [National Aborigines and Islanders Day Observance Committee] Week. People think NAIDOC Week is just for blackfellas. NAIDOC Week is a celebration for everybody, to celebrate Aboriginal culture and heritage. I think something like *Thalu* can be for everyone, black, white, or it doesn't matter who you are or where you from. It's teaching a story that everybody needs to know. Even though the Aboriginal Heritage Act within the government supposedly ranks Aboriginal Heritage as belonging to everybody in the state. Not just Aboriginal people. It's funny the government sees it that way but they don't treat it that way.

AA: How do you expect Indigenous and non-Indigenous audiences to experience the work differently? For example, do you think that it might be difficult for somebody that may have no cultural knowledge to be able to access the cultural complexity and richness of the work? Or are you making the work with the expectation that people will be able to understand how to navigate the different worlds and how to summon the spirits relating to them?

TM: Yeah. It could be the other way around, where instead of *Thalu* being the one to experience, if you've already looked at knowledge and that experience of Country, maybe it's the other way around where *Thalu* is the one that opens your eyes and you will go and seek that experience afterwards.

JH: It's interesting to see how you developed your storytelling and what was possible with it in VR. How did you get interested in working with VR? And what about VR did you find interesting?

TM: Myself and Justin [McArdle, Frame VR], met up for the first time

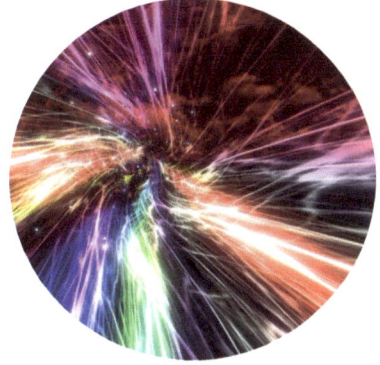

at a storytellers workshop conference down in Perth, where ScreenWest brought together Indigenous storytellers, filmmakers and writers together with people in the digital world: iPad comic makers, augmented reality developers and virtual reality stuff. I met Justin and he invited me down. He invited everyone down to his workshop in Perth. I was the only one that took his invitation. I went down there, had a couple of experiences in the virtual reality headset, with what they use, and used Tilt Brush for the first time. When you get into that virtual reality thing for the first time it always blows you away. I was blown away. He said, "Listen, make a story."

It took about a year to get talking and writing until we actually made something. I like doing my own thing. I love being creative. I thought virtual reality is a pretty new, creative way, of potentially telling an important story.

AA: Did you have in mind the story or the experience before choosing VR as the platform? As you also work in film, I'm curious to know what was the reason for choosing VR over film as your approach to tell this particular story?

TM: I sort of thought about it more as an experience, because I figured out that you could be sitting anywhere in the world with a virtual reality headset on. People all around the world could be transported to my Country. I thought that was special. I suppose it just shows the interest that I have in new technologies and telling stories in different ways because I've

made iPhone apps, traditional card games, web films and I've recorded music. I just like being creative in all types of different ways. Virtual reality - it's pretty cool.

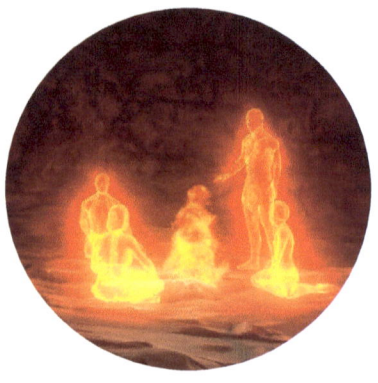

JH: You mentioned younger audiences coming in and learning about VR. When you were doing playtesting and development, was there anything where you were thinking about VR as a good medium for engaging a younger audience as much as an older audience?

TM: Yeah. We've had a setup in the community there, and we've had a number of kids, people of all ages actually, experiencing it. I think they really enjoyed the experience.

AA: Were there any obstacles that you found working in the medium different to film? There are different design challenges compared to film within VR.

TM: I was writing the story, getting the story was pretty much the same as film. I suppose not having the technical skill or not skill, but the know-how to work with the developers, where I think I'd develop it as we'd go along, because a couple of their first go's some of the scenes looked like very alien landscapes. They didn't look anything like in Pilbara. It was a little bit frustrating, because I'd send some stuff up. Like I'm saying, it didn't look like much. Only because they were having to build my Country, the landscape from scratch. There's no plug-ins that they can just plug in and create the Pilbara. Whereas film, obviously if you want some of the Pilbara you go and shoot it and you've got it straight away. A big challenge was time, I suppose. Taking a long time to create something that in my eyes, as a filmmaker, it's quite short, but as a developer, it's probably very hard.

JH: I noticed one thing that was quite interesting; when you first descend into the spiritual world, the way the player's attention was drawn to the bird through the trail that it left. Then it gives you a lot of time to know what you're supposed to be paying attention to, and the focus of the person who's in a VR environment. Were there any other things like that where the player can pretty much do whatever they want, but you need them to go through certain stages to progress the story?

TM: Yeah. With interaction, certain things like the rocks with the portals on it, they would pop up after a long time. We got them to pop up a bit faster.

AA: In film, directing your audience's experience happens three different times: over in the concept developing phase when you're writing a script, then when in production shooting, and then again, in the edit. Each time you are directing the audience's attention to affect in different ways, plotted through the linear experience of clocked time. How did you manage this process working with your developers to direct the user/player's experience?

TM: I'd probably start with the first thing, one of the hardest things about this project was it being made down in Perth and I'm up here. I couldn't see it every day. In saying that, when they would send a buildup to us, me and Stu [Stuart Campbell – Interactive Storyteller], we'd sit down and go through it a couple of times and write a whole list of notes about things we can improve on for the user experience, as you say. Yeah, we were conscious of not having people just stand around in each scene for too long for no reason. Even the directions from Jilly Jilly and the portals popping up a bit faster, and all those sorts of things. Comparing that to film, it was different.

JH: For me, having the human figure, with that amazing shade of their skin being this translucent sort of thing, standing in front of them felt pretty awesome. Having the suspense of standing in front of another human figure that you're interacting with works really well, because it's not just standing in front of someone, it's this bodily experience of being in the presence of that figure as well. Was Stu Campbell part of the development process, producing images that could then go to the developers to try and recreate that sort of work?

TM: Yeah, exactly like that, because Stu lives up here and we had talks about it. He drew these panels of each different world, what we wanted them to look like, similar to what they basically look like. He did more of a collage of illustration and Photoshop type images. That's basically what they used as guides to build these different scenes. They don't look exactly the same but they're pretty similar and have a similar, magical feel about them.

AA: What was your approach to using sound in the development and production?

TM: I got a hold of my follow-up here named Patrick, anything traditional and they use different kinds of stuff. I wanted it to be a more natural and magical sound. There's nothing musical, just atmospheric.

AA: I noticed the importance of sound, particularly in VR to draw people's attention, because you don't have the control of film-making. The film is a collective example of the importance of sound. It's half what you see and half what you hear. That includes the story, the narrative, the sound design of music, all the foley, all the various different layers of sound in film is quite significant in directing your experience, and through a particular timeframe. With VR, you can enter into this world and stay there forever. You've got more importance and reliance on sound to actually move you, direct your audience through space, and reveal those different worlds and so forth. I notice that the sound in *Thalu* is quite subtle with the use of birds and the natural sounds of Country were really beautiful. Was there a particular directorial approach that you took to using sound in this particular piece?

TM: I think I could have probably put more thought into it, even though you say it's beautiful sounding. I probably could have done a better job and enhanced the sound a bit more.

AA: Are there plans for further work, for further development?

TM: There should be. I personally don't think it's a final product at the moment. I don't think the sound is finished.

JH: As an Elder, you have certain knowledge and permission to tell these stories to a different audience. What did you decide could be shown and not? How do you work with telling certain things and being aware of what is inappropriate to show a general audience?

TM: I sort of just know. I don't always think about what the wider community or what the Elders would say, I just learn as I go what I can use. Even working in film, I do the same. I would not hesitate, but I sent the stories automatically to only allow things that I know old people, Elders would be happy with me showing. I still looked at them for cultural guidance and approval.

JH: Did you consult with Elders on this project?

TM: Yeah, a couple of my older cousins, talking with them about it. We're actually still working to show a few more. We're going to show it to a few elders before it's done, yeah.

AA: Do you feel an Indigenous approach to sharing knowledge came into how you told the story itself? The handing over and custodianship of knowledge and how that happens traditionally is quite different than Western ways. As there's a lot of cultural knowledge in this experience, did you consider that when designing the experience for players in *Thalu*?

TM: Yeah, I suppose in a way I don't really think too deeply about these things. I just write the story. Yeah, I don't write it with the beginning, middle and end, like a film. What I have written fits the idea of the virtual reality thing. I did feel when I was trying to write, it was hard to write, because I was thinking more about a film. When you write this sort of thing it's more of an experience. It is a learning experience for myself as well because like I say, it was not hard, but it was different trying to write for this, writing for a world, if you know what I mean. It turned out and acts differently to a short film. It was more a part of my process. The funding agency, they didn't really have any say on the creative side of it then.

They came a little bit later. They didn't guide me and they didn't give me any rules that I had to follow. Who knows, if they probably did then it may have turned out differently, because they probably would have wanted to see and hear things that they wanted to, just like a film. I think the funding agency funding this sort of VR experience, especially in WA, is brand new to them. I remember them saying "They've got this digital funding. What the hell do we do with it?" That's probably why I think it's where that initial storyteller and digital developer workshop came from. They had the money. They didn't know what to do with its funding for VR.

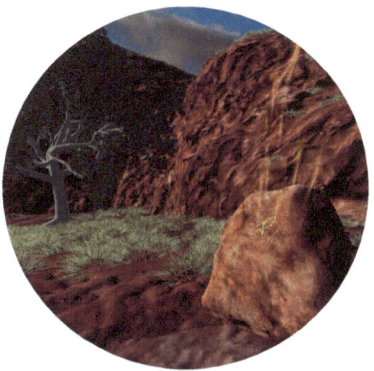

Screen Australia, they did the same. I remember I was part of a similar thing. I flew over to the east for a week-long workshop, where they had a cross-media lab. They had all these storytellers and filmmakers put together in a room with these fellows who taught you how to put a digital project together and pitch it. We spent a week together and then we pitched to ABC and NITV at the end of the week. I don't think any of us got any commissions out of that, but the one thing that did happen for me was at that workshop I developed my 'Welcome to Country' app into a pitch. I had that in the back of my mind and I eventually built that, separate from any of the state or federal funding. I did it myself.

JH: How do you advise people starting out in VR?

TM: The Screen West workshop was my first VR experience. I was seeing AR, augmented reality, before that or even at that workshop. For Virtual Reality, it was my first time.

AA: Have you got any desire to work with Augmented Reality?

TM: Yeah, augmented reality, I was trying to work with augmented reality a long time ago when it first came out. I was always interested with that, but I wanted to do more film projects with augmented reality, especially at Murujuga [on the burrup Peninsula], so maybe use AR to put up an augmented reality fence. You stand up and you can look around, or you can go, even pointing up, if you're on a rock art tool and importing out certain rock art that you can look at. There's all sorts of things. Even 360, when it first came out, actually in those crossover labs that we did over east, we came up with a pitch. It's been sitting there ever since. I've got a folder on my desktop full of digital ideas. One of them was using AR to identify all the traditional plants on the Morajoba or the Pilbara area here.

These things take time and money. Just recently, even last year, you find out someone has made those apps already. You can identify any plant right around the world, and you can download them. You can get all the scientific names, but you can't get the main uses and the cultural information. That's still a desire to do that.

JH: Do you have any advice to other storytellers who are starting out in AR, VR, digital media?

TM: Yeah. I'm always keeping an eye out on filmmaking initiatives and digital initiatives that Screen West and Screen Australia are always announcing. Then I've always got some sort of idea for a film or like I said, I've got a folder full of digital ideas as well. I suppose coming up with the ideas, like the way I write them out, I've learned that from attending those digital workshops over east, it's almost like writing a pitch. What does it do? What does it look like? Answering all those questions. This *Thalu* project, it got off the ground because I got sponsorship from a rock art foundation for it. Then *Frame VR* went and got the other half, based on I already had some money put towards it. If you want to do something, go and do it. Pitch yourself, I suppose. People know me as a filmmaker. A lot of other people know me as a musician. Some people know me as the fellow who made the iPhone app, the 'Welcome to Country' one. I suppose don't restrict yourself. Don't restrict yourself, but don't try and take too much as well.

JH: Would you say if you're starting out and you don't have any footholds don't wait until you get the opportunity before developing the ideas, just develop the idea into something that stands on its own, maybe find collaborators, then if any funding or any opportunities come along, you'll have something ready to show them?

TM: That's almost exactly the way I go, yeah. I've never met Justin or framed VR before, but I got invited to that workshop because I was a filmmaker, a storyteller.

AA: What do you have planned for after this project?

TM: Actually, I'm having more of a conversation with Stu. He's doing a documentary project, using a little bit of VR with some of the local kids here. He's got a bit of a crossover and an interesting project. Stu's doing all right with his augmented reality projects. He's got funding and he's opening up the augmented reality world to a lot of different artists. That's pretty interesting. He's getting more into virtual reality. *Thalu* was actually his first go with virtual reality. Now he's developing, he's probably one of the most sought-after virtual reality artists in Australia. He's been commissioned by everybody, from Disney to Google and YouTube and all that sort of stuff. I mention I've got a desire to continue using 360 video and virtual reality. Last year I went down to Perth and got my drone pilot's license. I want to do a lot more heritage work using the drones, creating all these 3D

images that you can make. I want to document Country using the drones, then make it into cultural maps before certain parts of my Country are destroyed by mining and all that. Using 360 cameras and drones on the ground.

I do these things with respect. We've always got these anthropologists and archaeologists coming into our communities, documenting our history and culture, and then taking off with it all somewhere down in a city a long way from us. By doing these different projects, like the *Thalu* VR project, this is documenting my language today and using it today. I'm not just documenting it, then creating an archive that my great-great grandkids might see one day. It's more about documenting it, saving it, using it today as well.

AA: Our culture is not static, it evolves.

TM: I think that's a tag on *Thalu*; *Dreamtime is now*. Today is my Dreamtime. People see Dreamtime as a thing of the ancient past but it's not. Today is my Dreamtime.

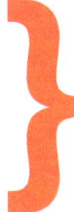

TORRES STRAIT VIRTUAL REALITY
RHETT LOBAN
(VIRTUAL REALITY)

Torres Strait Virtual Reality (TSVR) is a new and innovative way of learning and depicting a Torres Strait Islander experience. It provides access and insight into aspects of the Torres Strait culture, stories, customs, practices and viewpoints in a highly visual way through virtual reality. My game has sought to capitalise on the passions and enjoyment of video games held by our younger generation of adults and children to make learning a much more interesting journey. I hope TSVR has helped promote my community and the Torres Strait Islander culture to a wider audience and highlights our unique culture, traditions and history which few tend to know about. I provided the game as teaching material for several different and varying courses at the University of New South Wales engaging both Indigenous and non-Indigenous students to share our knowledge and foster understanding of cultural diversity.

TSVR illustrates Indigenous environmental knowledge of seasonal, plant and animal life cycles and how this aligns with the island surroundings like the stars, constellations and the wind. The game also depicts several cultural aspects and phenomena in the Torres Strait such as Tombstone openings, trade between Papua New Guineans and the Torres Straits Islanders, traditional hunting practices as well as characters from Torres Strait stories and legends.

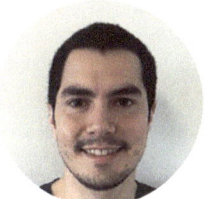

RHETT LOBAN
Creator / Researcher / Educator

Rhett Loban is an Associate Lecturer at the Department of Educational Studies at Macquarie University. He is also currently completing his PhD at the School of Arts and Media in the University of New South Wales. He is interested in the use of new and unconventional technology such as video games and virtual reality for learning and teaching. He is a Mainland Torres Strait Islander born in Brisbane whose father is from Thursday Island in the Torres Straits and mother is from Dundee in Scotland.

INTERVIEW

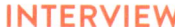

Josh Harle: Do you want to talk us through your project; the world and what the player would be doing in that space?

Rhett Loban: The game has different elements, but at its core, it's a cultural journey. In the Torres Straits, we have something called a Tombstone Opening. About a year or more after somebody has died, it depends on whether the family can afford it, after someone has passed away you have an end of a mourning period, but it's a little bit like a celebration with feasting and dancing and singing.

In the story, one of your family members has died and you're going to a Tombstone Opening on Thursday Island and you're going on a journey to get all these different items that you would need: drums, mats and spears for the ceremony and for the celebration. You're just going through and interacting with or encountering all these different things. When you go to one island you're looking for maybe drums or mats and they may not have them there, so you have to go to the next island. Then you have to get dugong and then turtle for the meat. In the game you get one at the reef and the other you can get near the beach. Typically you'd get it in the water but for the sake of gameplay we had some of the turtles on the beach. That's the journey, the cultural part.

There are other things in the game as well There's the Indigenous astronomy aspect, where you'll see the constellations in the sky and we've tried to make that quite authentic

in the position of where it's located. Those relate back to navigation, and the constellations would shift in the sky to indicate a different part of the season, which is also another indicator of events happening, like fish are getting fat or turtles are laying eggs.

Within the game different elements are interlinked, for example, the constellations themselves aren't just a bunch of stars; they represent different stories. Like in most cultures the constellations represent characters. One of the constellation characters you can find on one of the islands and you can encounter a mix of supernatural beings on islands as well. So there's a whole bunch of different elements that are there.

JH: One part of the game we find really interesting is that the tasks you have to perform are narrated to the player by your father's voice. So the cultural knowledge of the game is being taught possibly similar to how you learned it.

RL: Yeah, that's right. So he's basically guiding you through the journey, how you get from island to island. He's there and he is explaining the stories or his environmental knowledge, explaining everything.

Angie Abdilla: With the various stories within the astronomy, how is that experienced in the first person?

RL: You can either look up at the stars and you can see them there. Not all the stories that are in the stars are

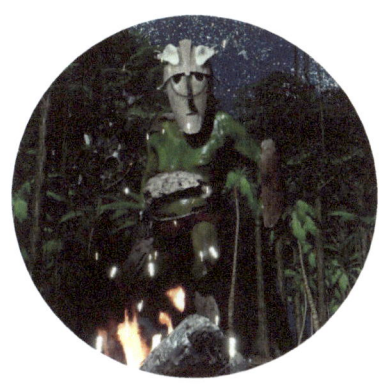

where he stole a turtle from people who had caught a turtle and then they ended up running off with the turtle and then he chases after them. But in the game you don't actually encounter that whole story, you only encounter elements of those stories.

JH: And from playing the game we've heard certain parts of the story told through the voice of your father guiding you in where to go and how to negotiate the spaces.

RL: Yeah, he is guiding you through and telling you how to navigate. Obviously, there is a mini-map there as well if you're lost, but my initial intention was that the stars would guide you and when you get to each check-point you would be told where you have to go next. The original intention is that you use the stars to navigate and find out where you need to go and there will be signing there to understanding the traditional navigation and constellations.

AA: What inspired you to create the experience, and who's the game for?

RL: I created the experience for a few different reasons. First off there wasn't really that much Torres Strait Island digital entertainment or digital media out there and even generally there's not even that much Indigenous media out there. So, I felt there was a gap and opportunity to contribute something to that space.

Another reason is VR was a new and trending thing that came out and I felt it was a very experiential platform

told on the ground, but we talk about the characters in the sky. So, we'll talk about Baidam the shark who's in the north or we'll talk about Tagai who's in the south. There are obviously stories behind that. Tagai was in his boat and there is a story about how he got there and he was travelling with maybe 12 or 13 other people and they did something bad and betrayed him. He ended up killing them and then, if you look at the opposite side sky of the sky, they are represented there, like 12 or 13 stars. So, there are stories like that, but perhaps they are not illustrated as completely as I would've liked to in the game journey.

You are told parts of the stories, but there are other stories that are there. So you're not told the entire story, but you encounter characters within the stories, or you encounter elements of those stories' journey. There's another story, it's a giant called Wawa and if you go to one of the more north-western islands you'll encounter Wawa. But that in itself is a story on its own 'cause there's a whole thing

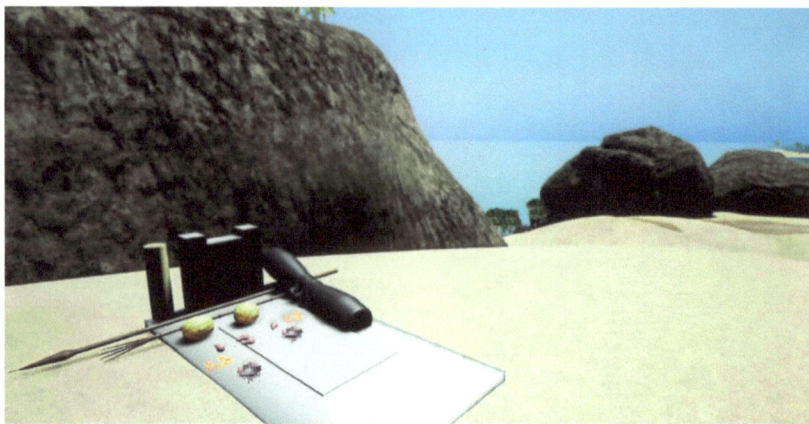

to do justice to the way Torres Strait Islander or Indigenous people might have passed down knowledge. Astronomy is a very visual thing, you look up at the stars and you can see the stars. You're putting on these goggles and you're looking around and you're being immersed in that space. I felt the way that knowledge has been passed on and the way that it's been done in the past at least, it's very true to that sort of medium.

Other reasons would be practical in that I had the ability to make it myself. I had learnt maybe a year before how to work with *Unreal Engine 4*, so I thought "Oh what do I need to do" and the transition from just taking it from a game to VR game. Technically it's not a big thing, but in terms of design, there are obviously bigger complications. I found that out while I was doing it. I had the ability and it was much cheaper and accessible to get the technology and to create the game.

AA: What were the complications specific to working in VR? Design or conceptual?

RL: It's got to do with VR in general. There are other people that have come out with games, and you know you can have your user interface and there are general things that you can have. But VR is this new weird thing around the world - it's an open world to teleport. Like SkyRim VR, they basically just teleport around the map. I don't necessarily really like that, so I thought a controller would be good, but this brings in issues because there is a disconnect between what the people are doing in the world and what they are actually seeing. There were issues around that and working in VR. A lot of people had trouble with the journey as opposed to if you created a generic, normal non-VR first-person game.

JH: Maybe you can give more of an overview of the journey, to help explain why it's so much about travelling between these different islands. Why would you say the teaching is so much about different places and that journey, especially in the context of the ceremony where you have to go to the different places and pick up different things? Why just sitting in a room with your Dad telling you a story is not the same learning experience.

RL: Generally moving between the islands, I guess it's something that's unique to the Torres Straits. I'm born in Brisbane, from the mainland, and my father is actually from Thursday Island, but if you trace my ancestry back it comes from two different islands. We have ancestry from Mabuiag Island which is in the west and then we have ancestry from Boigu Island which is north. If you look at some of the Torres Strait Islands, there's relationships and there's things that go between those islands. It's important because even though we're from Thursday Island and Thursday Island's the commercial hub or the administrative hub, a lot of our ancestry goes back to these different islands.

Traditionally within the Torres Straits were certain language groups and people know you're from certain islands, but we all identify as a unified people. So, going to the islands it kinda tells you that there's the whole islands. It's just not by itself, there is a whole area and it's all interconnected and linked in different ways. So, even when you go to the first island, you're trading with them, so it's not just you're on your island and that's

it. I think even in the game itself it's interesting to go from one place to another. Like ideally something I really would've have liked, but I didn't have the time or the resources was to really make each island unique, 'cause if you go to some of the islands some of them won't have that much vegetation, they might be made of coral clay or it is a very rocky island. On Duan Island that's where people go to learn how to use dynamite to practice for quarrying and mining. So each island has their own characteristic and there is something unique or different on each island.

JH: In mainstream games, the experience of travelling between different places and especially that environment with islands you normally get from games like *Far Cry* is where your engagement with those different spaces is being a basically insidious invading force. The reason why you're going between those different points is that you're attacking this thing on this one and attacking this thing on this one. Or the idea of a home, you know you might start out in a valley, which is where you're from and then be forced through whatever dramatic reason to travel to these different locations. I think it's fairly unique to have something where you're traveling through different places not as an invader or not as someone whose exploring this place that's new as an outsider, but for there to be a sense of your background intricately woven between all of those different locations. So its distributed amongst all of these different places.

AA: Would you describe it as almost like a cultural mapping process? The way in which you're navigating through the experience, being directed through the various different islands, it's not, as Josh's said, in pursuit of the all mighty conquer, or the pursuit of mass killing. It's something radically different.

RL: So, typically when we think of native title we think of things like land rights, but it's also your right to exercise like cultural practices on the land as well, and the angle that they took on that was that, 'cause you're going on a Tombstone Opening to get all these different things you'll get Papua New Guinea drums and spears from Papua New Guineans that come over. You know Australia is separate from Papua New Guinea, so there typically would be a border and you'd have to go through that, because those cultural practices were in place before colonization, there was a treaty to facilitate that.

That might be something that could be seen as a native title journey to continue those cultural practices or if it's something like hunting dugong or turtle, which is within the context of doing it for, 'cause that's how we sustain ourselves and we don't necessarily have access to fresh meat. That's within the context of this Tombstone Opening, like the celebratory sort of thing. It's something that we've done and that we've always done so that's another stance that you can look at it from the journey.

The way that they looked at it in the education class, was from the process of creating the game. So, here I can go through the protocols that you have to adhere to when you're making any sort of product or if you're in a community, there are certain things you have to do. It's no different if you're making a product either. Going to an Elder on board or consulting different Torres Strait Islanders. I went to general Indigenous organizations as well to see what they thought and then I'd go ask parts of my family and tried to get consent there too. They were looking at it like, if you're doing anything with any Indigenous content it's just being respectful about it and understanding there are certain protocols for different people.

So I think that's the way that they were looking at it 'cause it's a game, it's something different from just going into a community.

JH: Would you say it's more than documentation because there is a potential for works to be more than a transliteration of culture into a form of documentation? Let's say you can make the case that your experience reflects the way of teaching knowledge, and the way in which maybe you would have learnt about it through your Dad telling, through travelling between those different islands, the fact that that way of teaching is built into spaces, means that it's actually practised culture so that its generating new cultural knowledge in itself?

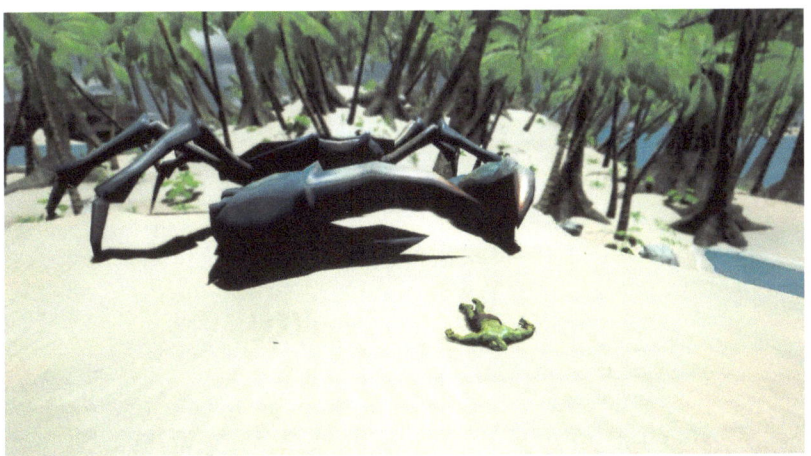

RL: Yeah, absolutely. One of the things, at least in the Torres Straits, for some Torres Strait islanders culture is perceived as a tree. So you have these roots at the bottom and these are like traditional or age-old knowledge and it feeds up into the tree and out of this comes new branches and these new branches for me it's kinda like new forms of art and new forms of expression. But the branches themselves don't represent the exact thing underneath.

So it's a weird mix of something new, but it still in its essence has something old or something back to tradition there. So yeah, that's the way that I would see my game, is that it's this new branch that's coming out and there are familiar elements there, but it's not gonna be completely a representation or a complete look back, there are new things in there as well.

Even with the characters, I had to make do with what I could, like the Dogai. The Dogai is a witch and she's on the islands. So, in one of the stories she must jump into the ocean as she turns into an octopus so I was thinking how could I represent with maybe these generic models? How could I represent something like that? So I knew that sticking in an octopus and covering her in shells and all sorts of other things. No, but that's not what a Dogai looks like or at least not what artists in the books say what a Dogai looks like. But nobody really knows because it's their own interpretation journey so it's just what people think.

JH: Super interesting to talk about that process of telling the stories in a different medium and how you negotiated that. It may be interesting to think, was that part of the consultation as well, where you were talking through with other people about what would be an appropriate way to represent these characters?

RL: Yeah, well I think that was me also discussing with my dad because the way that the Dogai is represented in the story is that they have really big ears. They use these to cover themselves, to disguise themselves as a rock or to do different things. So this was one thing that was there, but we built a model for the ear, but it didn't really work. It was just like a solid object and it stuck out. It didn't really act like a big ear would act, because when you think of the big ear, you might think it might flop down and then it might wave around and do stuff. We didn't have the capacity to build in animation and do all these different intricate sorts of things. So we just took creative license and said, okay well what are the other, what's the story about. Then we were thinking, how do we build elements and what would it look like if it was in that?

I was talking with my dad because he's the one who... he tells me the stories. So I have knowledge of the stories, but he's the person that has them all. The ones that we read about, that's another thing itself. Obviously, we also get it from other places, but we thought, if it's like that, then maybe we can have an octopus because he goes into the ocean and then shells. Or, if it's the Dogai from the guinea bird's nest, or guinea fowl, it's a bird, but they live in this big mound. Then, normally in the mound, they have things sticking out of it, like leaves or palm leaves or something like that. So then we thought, for the Dogai, we can put it covered in leaves. So there was a discussion with my dad about

that and then interweaving those elements into it as well, I think.

AA: You've mentioned before that there's a different story when you're reading texts to research cultural information as opposed to the process of your Dad sharing these stories. Can you describe your research process?

RL: Yeah, so we get a lot of myths from looking up things on the internet. What they used to do is they used to have a lot of books. So we looked at lots of books, and everyone has their own depiction of what a Dogai would look like, so that gives you an idea, but when they're telling you the stories, it's obviously your own imagination and it's something working, and it's something different. So I guess, if I'm told the stories, I have my own vision of what it might be like, but a lot of the stories overlap or they're not consistent. There's variations between them, but the stories are out there. So the ones that he does tell me, you also find in the book as well.

I guess the difference would be, if I'm told the stories, I have my own idea of what it might be like, but if you read it, then you obviously think about the picture and how it all comes out.

JH: There's an interesting element of your VR where it's your dad talking you through the things you have to do as part of the ceremony. So how do you think it's important for teaching this cultural practice. Your character in the game is Indigenous, regardless of whether the actual person playing or experiencing the game is from an Indigenous background or not. The character that you're playing is someone who's part of this culture, related to the family member who's died, with an Elder talking through these things. It's not too dissimilar from games like *Grand Theft Auto* [GTA] where you're put into a position of a particular character with a background very different from the majority of people who'd normally be playing that game. Do you want to talk about that experience and how it would work for teaching as a way of communicating that culture maybe?

RL: By being placed there. Yeah, I guess, like you said, because you're placed there. You're immersed in the culture and you're having to go through the cultural, if there is such a thing like this cultural process of the Tombstone Opening and going through those different elements, into the different islands to collect and do different things.

AA: Was it a consideration when you were designing the experience, that the personal experience was adopting your persona, your experience?

RL: I never thought of it that way, but now that you say it, I guess it is something maybe akin to that. We originally actually did have a story set out. So you would take, I think the guy, we might have named him, his name was Gith I think. The original story, he's from Mabuiag Island, which is the island that you start on, and he's going to the tombstone on the Thursday Island. So you actually do have the character, but there's no real

exploration of the character's story or anything there. So, in essence, you are put in this place and you're not told much about the character's background and there isn't that much there I guess. You could see it as my experience to some extent, but I never really intended it that way. It was just that you were in this person and you just had to go through this cultural journey and you encountered all these different things on the way.

AA: How are the interactive elements of the experience important in telling the story or the work?

RL: I think it probably worked more into the natural world. The understanding, the natural science or the environmental science. Those are probably the more interactive things that change in the environment, and tell you about the place or the islands, I think. So, as I said, when you get to one checkpoint, I try to integrate a tidal system where the tides will rise up and down depending on the day and night cycles. It must be every day, so 24 hours, the tide rises four times, every time. It doesn't do it at the same level. It goes up and down, but it might go higher, like really high, and then very low, and then a little bit higher, and then a little bit lower, and it goes back up to high again. So that's one of the interactive elements that I've put into the game to try and maybe illustrate the different issues or environmental things that affect people on the islands.

For example, when you go up onto the beach, you may have to wait for the tide to go down, or for the second tide to come up before the boat can actually take off. Or it might be something like, you have to move the boat out far enough, because if you don't move it out far enough, then you're going to be stuck on that island or stuck on a sandbar for like 24 hours until it comes back up again enough. That's one of the interactive elements. Then, the other thing would be, when you get to a certain checkpoint, there's a change in the seas, so you'll see a shift in the stars or in a constellation that tells you what's happening. So I think the interactive elements there, that change based on the player's behaviour, is more of the environmental sort of stuff. You encounter the supernatural beings and all of that, and you're told the stories, but it's not like they chase you around or do stuff like that. Most of the interaction, I feel, comes out of the environmental knowledge.

AA: On arriving in the game, are there instructions guiding your purpose for your mission?

RL: So you're basically guided by my dad's voice. So that's where you're getting a lot of the instructions from, being guided by the voice. Like I said, you have a mini-map there, but it's basically going through and the voice is telling you these pieces of knowledge or where you have to go to next and maybe the significance of why you need to get there and what will happen when you get there and what you need to watch out for.

JH: From memory, it starts with a place in the context of an explanation of the overarching goal you're trying to do, getting these items for the ceremony.

RL: Yeah, it explains what a Tombstone Opening is. It explains like you said, why you're going to all these different places and what you'll need to get. I think I've even placed a tombstone at the beginning to illustrate the purpose of the journey as well.

JH: When you're talking about building this game, you talk about things like representation and how you want to represent different figures, but what does it mean to have this world and these actions represented in VR? Did you need to take extra care to communicate something? Did you actually show any real person represented in the VR experience? How did you explain what the implications of having it in VR as a game would be to the way that it was communicated?

RL: The way that I actually see it, because it's an educational material, I actually don't see it any different to, say, a *PowerPoint* presentation or some sort of educational or learning material like that, that any other lecturers or educators have made. I would say it obviously has a lot more steps than any other lecture material would. I got my Dad on board. I talked to a lot of my family. I showed different Torres Strait Islanders and other Aboriginal people the game and I consulted with two other Indigenous organizations as well.

So I've gone through a lot to do it, but

the way that I basically see it is, it's still an educational medium. If I was to go commercial, or I took it into a different sphere. People asked me whether I wanted to exhibit it at the library. I thought maybe that's okay at the beginning, but then it's taking it somewhere else, because people charge money to get into the library. So then it's charging money for something, so it becomes an entirely different beast when you start doing that. So the way that I've always seen it is it's educational material, it's really no different, only the way that it's presented. If the content is the same and you reference people or if you cite people or something like that, it's no different. But I obviously still went and took a lot of precautions because that's the protocol as well, but I still did all those sorts of things because that's just the respectful thing to do and it's covering myself. So there were extra precautions I took, but in the end, it's teaching material.

JH: So, if you're talking about it in the context of this, you have already some control over how it's framed and how people have to have some sort of framed experience of it and you have some control over the knowledge and who is getting access to that knowledge and the context in which it's happening. Can you talk more to that?

RL: Some people from Nura Gili at UNSW were really good and they were on board with the game. Then, I'm a part of another organization called Indigitek. It's basically getting Indigenous students involved in STEM

[Science Technology Engineering Mathematic] related career paths or interests. So I actually did a presentation of the game at one of their events. So they were on board and they were giving a little bit of feedback about that as well. So people from there. So those were the two organizations, but then again, I'm talking with different people.

I'm talking to different people in my family. Including in the Torres Straits, so there's people even back there. Then, another Torres Strait Islander down here in Sydney played it down here. So we're still talking with different people and getting feedback and going through the protocol and the process.

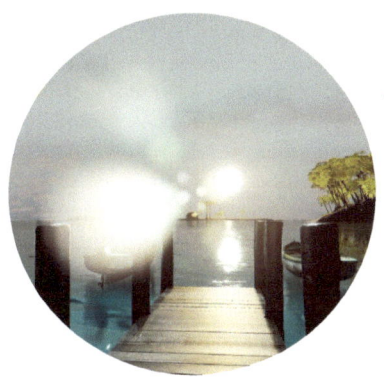

JH: I'm curious about how you handle the potential misuse of the technology, what the consequences of making this would be, and how you communicate these possibilities to members of the community when you are seeking permission. Say you put it out for free, for example, so it wasn't

so much an issue of the commercial benefit or the financial benefit that you might get from this, but just the fact that there was no control over what was being put out there, the potential for misuse, you don't have any control over how people read or use the work.

So, for example, all you have to do is look at things like GTA videos where the power to move around the space and use it in your own way is something that allows people to do things like create their own meaning from the way in which they interact with that game. As funny as it is to see people tea-bagging in an FPS game, where you kill someone and then make your avatar rub itself suggestively on them.

All of these ways where people can be completely irreverent to the original point of the game. That's just funny to see it in a commercial game where the significance of it is just there for entertainment, but the possibility of that in something that is more of a serious game, more communicating something that's important, is definitely there, I would say. People are amazingly good at inventing new ways of being irreverent, it's difficult to speculate.

On the basis of what people do to games at the moment, the field is completely open to that. Just things like killing off important story characters in a game and celebrating the violence if you can figure out how to perpetrate in a game is something that you don't have any control over.

It's hard to speculate, as I say. It's like the set up of, well, how much can people be assholes. The idea is people are amazingly innovative in the way that they would be assholes, especially with a medium that allows such a level of creation of meaning through a practice of the space. How much do you try to communicate these possibilities to participants and Elders? Yeah, it's an open question.

RL: You can't control people in what they do. It's just like you said. They'll come up with new ways or the most creative ways to mess up something. I can create the game and people can abuse it. There's always that vulnerability. The vulnerability could be a video being read different, they can overlay stuff on a video and put different silly things in there, or they can put voice-overs or stuff like that. So I guess there is that opportunity for people to abuse a game or put it in a negative light or something like that. I can't control the people. It's just me putting my thing out there and that just carries the risk of that. If people are disrespectful, then that's their own issue, or they need to sort themselves out.

I think if I was to go commercial, and I did release this, I'd actually be targeting schools. I'd be targeting educational institutions because that's where this would go. I've just got the *Oculus Store* [to share VR games] so I might even do something on that in the future. So I might put it on the *Oculus Store* or something, but the real people I'd be targeting would be primary school and then high schools, and then maybe some University stuff. Those are the places I would be going.

AA: Are there any plans in place to do that?

RL: I haven't done anything yet. I'm talking with a couple of people but I'd ideally like to release something maybe in more of a mobile app as opposed to the current one, mostly because it's more accessible and it will get it out there. I haven't done anything yet, but I plan to do that. So maybe in the near future, I'll have something and I can do that. I was thinking I might do, instead of doing a big game, I might do modules. So I'll focus on one particular element, so one thing might be astronomy. In the game, if you go into the ocean, you can actually see crayfish migration happening as well. So I thought that might be another cool thing. Then, there's a couple of things there that I want to do. So that will be in the future.

JH: You said that you got introduced to *Unreal*. How did you originally get introduced to the medium?

RL: I think I must have played something. I went somewhere and I must have played something and I thought it was really good. Then I thought, I might have a VR, so I got it and I started making a game and then I was able to make something. So I got into game making through the class that I had to teach, but I can't remember what I played. I must have played it somewhere. I thought

it was really cool and then I thought, oh okay, maybe I can make something like this.

JH: For most people, from the creative background, it will be a question of how did you get into the technology. If you're coming from more of the technology side, with the competency of doing that, maybe the question should be how did you start thinking about using it as a culture of storytelling process?

RL: I think it will probably go back to the thing that I was talking about in the beginning. Nobody's really done anything about Torres Strait Island or Indigenous games in general. There's not really that much out there. There are some things like depicted as one-offs in the game or maybe yeah, there's maybe little bits of things in there, but nothing really substantial. So I thought, oh it's a story not really told. I think there's some interesting things about the environment to be said. So that's how I started seeing it in that way, is that there is nothing really there, so why not talk about it.

JH: Do you have anything in mind for inspiring examples of digital media work that helped you think about what you're working on now? Even if it's not specifically Indigenous, is there something in any particular way that you're like, this is working really well?

RL: You mean something I saw that's from a non-western perspective that I liked or something like that? Yeah, I know there are obviously some things

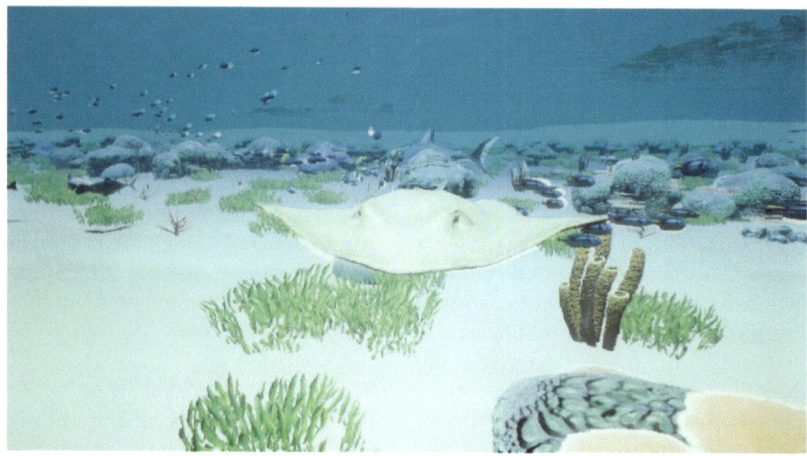

out there. There's a lot of Native American ones out there. So I think like *Assassin's Creed*, in one of them you play a Native American. There was another one, I think it's like an Inuit girl and she has a fox [*Never Alone (Kisima Ingitchuna)*]. That one was quite well received, but there's not really that many that I've played. Most of the games that I actually play are more grand strategy games.

They're probably, talking about western perspectives, they're probably the worst type because they're built around the idea of empire and conquest and expanding and colonizing.

JH: But as you've said you can at least do alternate histories with those?

RL: You can. In fact, I even made a mod, and I inserted Indigenous people into there as well. Even then, it's still hard to play. It's a good game

because it opens you up to the idea of understanding different people around the world and people you wouldn't have otherwise known about if you didn't have access to this big map. At heart, it's still a very Eurocentric game where it's all focused on Europe and expansion through conquering as opposed to maybe through building tall. You can do it, but it's easier to just expand now.

JH: I think we talked before about how I play *Civilization*, where I just stay in a little spot and develop all the technology and culture that I can, and then die basically because the militaristic other nations come and take over. That's my ideal, just sitting there developing science and culture. So working on this project is a very distinct difference between that colonial strategy game perspective and what you've been doing?

RL: Yeah, it's very different. In some ways, I've obviously inserted Torres Strait Islanders into the game, but I guess, if you're looking at it at a super realistic level or way, in some ways it may be hard to represent those people in those things, because the way that those games work is that there are like states and then you can control the state. Some Indigenous people have that, so we did have that in the Torres Straits. There were islands that people controlled and land was passed down, but in some ways, it's still hard to reflect that view or the way that the people are represented through the journey. So maybe a VR view to me is more a representation of Indigenous culture, than a grand strategy game.

JH: That's a really excellent point of comparison and reason for using VR.

RL: That's the contrast that I would see is that, even though I love those games and I try to put it in, it's still hard to reflect them in some sense. Do you know what I mean?

JH: Yeah, that's a really good answer. Also, you mentioned, and I'd completely forgot to follow up, that one difficulty in developing your environment is the fact that there's prefab models of all of these sort of western characters and objects that, for you, when you had to create it all from scratch. So it was actually a massive effort to create representations of people and things, because they're just not part of this library that everyone has access to.

RL: Yeah, that's right. So when you play the game, you will not find any people models in there because tropical islands are like everywhere in the world. Or there's vegetation or there's sea creatures or deer or boars or whatever. They're all generic models and they're everywhere, but even just creating a simple generic sphere or drum took a while, but from what is in my budget. I could have gotten my students to help me. You're almost better off buying the models as opposed to creating them yourselves, because there's so much effort involved in that. So yeah, I deliberately steered clear of any people models, because there wasn't anyone there that looked appropriate, because the Torres Strait Islanders are a mix of different people, you'll typically find they look quite Melanesian. There's nothing there that really represents Torres Strait Islanders in the islands if you went there now, what they would typically look like.

So, in some ways, I feel I didn't have anyone there. There were African Americans there, but they're not the same people because they're all dressed up. They dress differently. They're like in business suits and I'd have to have someone walking around in a business suit!

AA: You say it's more beyond the cultural artefacts that you didn't have access to, to tell the story most accurately. Would you say it's more of an issue to get the intention and purpose of the game, and the direction all the users experience, because, essentially, the cultural artefacts all have a huge amount of assumptions built into them and only represent a tiny part of the world's culture. So how much did that hold you back as opposed to getting the user experience down pat?

What were the obstacles you overcame creating a culturally rich experience that's different to this first person, very Eurocentric, conquest type experience that games are renown for? How did the lack of access to culturally appropriate artifacts impact on the development process?

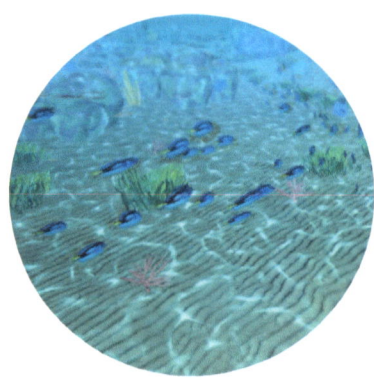

RL: Obviously because I couldn't access the authentic weaponry or even just drums it definitely impeded what I could and couldn't put in. To some extent, it did determine the way that it went, in the way that I designed the game, but to some extent, it didn't. If I had people there, it might have affected it and it made it more realistic. Some of the comments that we got from the people in the feedback is that they wanted people in the world and they wanted people

to inhabit the world. I couldn't do that, so I didn't put them in, but I think, if I were to put them in, it would change the experience, but I wouldn't have to shift all of my stuff around to change it for those people. So it didn't impede what I was doing, but it would have made a better experience.

AA: The purpose is your relational experience to the environment that you're in. That's more important than the focus on the quest and the cultural artefacts that you're collecting.

RL: Oh, this experience in general. Yeah, the travelling and going to each place, and then seeing the different things. I think, yeah, that's probably more important than something small or maybe.

AA: It comes back to your relationship with, and understanding of how you're connected with everything, like the tides and the stars. It feels like it was the priority, as opposed to getting hung up on the fact that you don't have access to the-

RL: The models or stuff like that?

AA: Yeah, yeah.

RL: Yeah, that's right. So the game experience in itself, that's core and I think that's the thing with most games, isn't it. It's designing that experience and all the aesthetics that you add later. That adds to it. There is something like having the authenticity there to make it really nice and feel really realistic and unique and authentic to its own thing but, in itself, it's the experience and going through it. Yeah, I think you're right. It's probably more the process in going through it that's more of a cultural experience as opposed to necessarily all the aesthetics that would be there. It adds to it and it would have been way better if I did have it, but I still happened to make a game without it.

JH: The reason why I'm particularly interested in this is because it speaks to Ramsey Nasser's writing about programming in a non-English language basically. The idea is that, though it is possible to do it, there's a huge hidden cost to try and do things counter to what the dominant culture of producing these things is. So, yes, you can program in Arabic, but basically, you don't have to have access to any of these libraries that you would normally use, which doesn't make it technically impossible but it makes it very, very difficult and you need to fight against that.

It's very interesting to think that there's this hidden extra effort you need to go into to tell you're own stories because what you're working against is basically a landscape of all of this stuff that's reproduced over and over again. Over representations of western history, over millennia of ancient pottery up to what have you, suits and things like that, that you just don't have access to the equivalent of. I find that deeply interesting as something to make people aware of. Related to that, do you have any advice to people starting out using this medium for telling their stories?

RL: You really have to think about the story or the game that you're going to have, because I think some games just flat out won't work or some ways of storytelling or some ways of doing things in the game may not work. So I think my game, to some extent, didn't really work, to some extent because of the way that you use the control. About 30% of the people got sick. So, that's a huge part of my audience that I lost just by using the controls.

They get sick at different times. Some would be two minutes, some would be fifteen minutes, others could play for an hour, but there were a group of people that would be consistently getting sick. I think the later class groups, there wasn't really that issue. We started getting people, maybe only a few people that started getting sick. When you play VR, depending on, typically for the high-end VR, there's some sort of disconnect between what the person's body is doing and what they're seeing. So even though they're moving in the game, they're not moving their bodies, so I think there's something there, like they get dizzy. It varies. People react differently. Some people get sick and they get dizzy. Other people start sweating a lot, and I mean a lot, and you can see sweat coming down off them or you put it on and you can feel it. So people react differently to it, depending on what it is.

I feel like it's hard to say. Even, I think the way that you react in the game is different to how you would move around in the world. So, say in a game, you can run right up to a wall or you can run up to a tree or something like that, but if you were running around, you wouldn't run up to a tree and then put it straight up to your face. You wouldn't run into a tree or run through it or something like that. And people got sick when they did that, when they either ran into the tree or through the tree or into a rock or something, because you wouldn't do that in real life. Something like that.

Then, there might be issues like, in the beginning, it could be a testament to VR, but in the beginning, we had the water and you put the boat on the water, but there was a setting to make the waves choppy. So, when you got in, it was so choppy that it started moving around like you really were on a boat, and then you get sick straight away and you'd have to take it off. So there'd be stuff like that that you'd have to be ultra aware of as well. It

could be a testament to how good VR is! So we had to put those down, but there's just certain stuff in VR that doesn't work or your body is different from what you're experiencing and what you do in the game would be different from how you would do it in real life. So then, in some sense, it might be good to have a teleportation thing, where you teleport around. Then, of course, it breaks the emersion of being inside that game.

JH: Some of it, I'd say, is around design of that relationship to space. It's totally necessary for yours to be able to move through big open spaces. When you see things like *Fallout 4 VR*, where they've retrofitted this huge commercial game for VR, it's disappointing to see that they haven't thought about what that requires. They do things that are basically blacklisted from design of VR. In

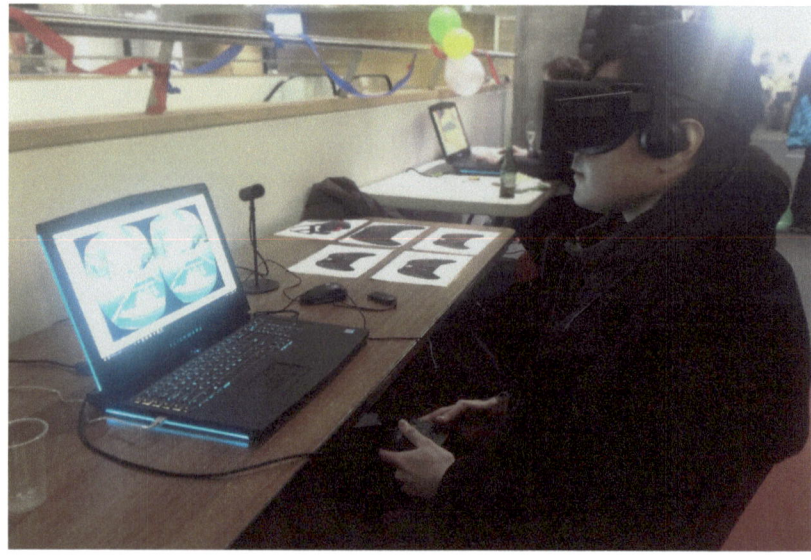

room-scale VR the position of the players head is matched one to one with the position in space, and when you walk around and move your head everything feels attached as if you're in that space. *Fallout* do things like, if you walk up to something and look over it, there's a collision boundary over it, and it will just sickeningly push you away from the object without your control. They spent millions of dollars developing this thing. I guess we can take heart that, even with a millions of dollars budget, people can mess up their design of the VR interaction.

RL: If you just consider those sorts of things about what would work and what doesn't work it definitely helps. It may also have to do with people just being new to the technology. I can remember maybe twenty years ago, or ten, fifteen years ago, people would get plane sick a lot. I don't think I've ever seen anyone get plane sick now. I don't think I've ever seen anyone use the paper bag to vomit into. I'm sure there are exceptions, but I don't think I've ever seen anyone get plane sick now. So maybe the technology is different or we've become accustomed to the technology. That's a possibility.

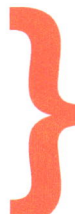

NOTES, FIGURES, AND BIBLOGRAPHIES

INTRODUCTION NOTES

1. Yellow Bird, M. 2008, 'Postscript - Terms of Endearment: a Brief Dictionary for Decolonizing Social Work with Indigenous Peoples', in M. Gray, J. Coates & M. Yellow Bird (eds), *Indigenous social work around the world towards culturally relevant education and practice*, Ashgate, Aldershot, Hants, England; Burlington, VT from Hromek, Danièle. 2017, *'Impact' catalogue essay*, UTS Art, Sydney, Australia

2. See *Collisions* showcase for a project which discusses the Aboriginal Australian side of this technology.

3. Turnbull, David. (2005). *Masons, Tricksters and Cartographers: Comparative Studies in the Sociology of Scientific and Indigenous Knowledge.* London and New York, Routledge, p2.

4. Amnesty International. "This is what we Die For: Human Rights Abuses in the Democratic Republic of the Congo Power the Global Trade in Cobalt." (2016). Retrieved from https://www.amnestyusa.org/files/this_what_we_die_for_-_report.pdf

5. Bronton, C. "Rare-earth mining in china comes at a heavy cost for local villages." *The Guardian* 7 (2012). Retrieved from https://www.theguardian.com/environment/2012/aug/07/china-rare-earth-village-pollution

6. Ngai, Pun, and Jenny Chan. "Global capital, the state, and Chinese workers: the Foxconn experience." *Modern China 38*, no. 4 (2012): 383-410. Retrieved from http://content.csbs.utah.edu/~mli/Economics%205420-6420/Ngai%20and%20Chan-Global%20Capital%20State%20and%20Chinese%20Workers.pdf

7. Heidegger, Martin. "The question of technology and other essays." Trans. W. Lovett. New York: Harper and Row (1977).

A PERSONAL COMPUTER NOTES

---

1. Available at: https://github.com/ocornut/imgui/blob/
fe5347ef94d7dc648c237323cc9e257aff6ab917/imgui_draw.cpp#L2666

2. Available at: https://github.com/mrdoob/three.js/blob/
f81506e172571ab106d0164530bbc1a4802fc2d4/src/extras/core/Font.js#L63

3. Available at: https://docs.spring.io/spring/docs/2.5.x/javadoc-api/org/springframework/aop/
framework/AbstractSingletonProxyFactoryBean.html

A PERSONAL COMPUTER FIGURES

Figure 1: Pokemon Go screenshot (Nassar, 2016), accessed from: https://nopenotarabic.tumblr.
com/post/149021392583/a-wild-pok%C3%A9mon-go-appeared-it-used-common-arabic

Figure 2: Pepsi Ad screenshots (Nassar, 2017), accessed from: https://nopenotarabic.tumblr.
com/post/159231568203/nothing-says-love-like-butchering-a-language

"SHUT UP AND PLAY" NOTES

1. Sean Cubitt, *Digital aesthetics* (London: Sage, 1998).

2. Carly Kocurek, *Coin-operated Americans: Rebooting boyhood at the videogame arcade* (Minneapolis: University of Minnesota Press, 2015).

3. Graeme Kirkpatrick, *The formation of gaming culture: UK games magazine 1981-1995* (London: Palgrave, 2015).

4. Mia Consalvo, "The monsters next door: Media constructions of boys and masculinity." *Feminist Media Studies 3*, no. 1 (2003): 27-45. Kirkpatrick, *The formation of gaming culture.*

5. Anastasia Salter and Bridget Blodgett, "Hypermasculinity & Dickwolves: The contentious role of women in the new gaming public." *Journal of Broadcasting & Electronic Media*, 56, no.3 (2012): 401-416.

6. Eron Gjoni, *The Zoë Post* [web log] (2014, August 16). Archived at https://thezoepost. wordpress.com/

7. Maya Oppenheim, "Jessi Slaughter on becoming a meme and falling victim to trolls after infamous YouTube video." *Independent* (2016, March 31). . Retrieved from http://www. independent.co.uk/news/people/jessi-slaughter-youtube-video-viral-troll-damien-leonhardt-2010-myspace-a6959436.html

8. Shira Chess and Adrienne Shaw, "A Conspiracy of Fishes, or, How We Learned to Stop Worrying About #GamerGate and Embrace Hegemonic Masculinity." *Journal of Broadcasting & Electronic Media*, 59, no. 1 (2015): 212.

9. Chess & Shaw, "A Conspiracy of Fishes," 209.

10. Doxxing: publishing an individual's private information, such as address and phone number, on the internet, allowing for effectively anonymous harassment in the real world.

11. Swatting: hoax call to emergency services citing gun-crime, which sends an armed response (SWAT team) to the victim's address. These can have fatal consequences.

12. Daniel Golding and Leena Van Deventer, *Game changers: From Minecraft to misogyny* (Melbourne: Affirm Press, 2016): 169-173.

13. Adrienne Massanari, "#Gamergate and The Fappening: How Reddit's algorithm, governance, and culture support toxic technocultures." *New Media & Society*, 19, no. 3 (2017): 334.

14. Abby Ohlheiser, "Why 'social justice warrior,' a Gamergate insult, is now a dictionary entry." *The Washington Post* (2015, October 7). Retrieved from https://www.washingtonpost.com/news/the-intersect/wp/2015/10/07/why-social-justice-warrior-a-gamergate-insult-is-now-a-dictionary-entry/?utm_term=.495ac40f9757

15. Kishonna L. Gray, Bertan Buyukozturk, and Zachary G. Hill (2017). "Blurring the boundaries: Using Gamergate to examine 'real' and symbolic violence against women in contemporary gaming culture." *Sociology Compass*, 11, no. 3 (2017), 1-8.

16. Golding and Van Deventer, *Game changers.*

17. Adrienne Shaw, "The Internet Is Full of Jerks, Because the World Is Full of Jerks: What Feminist Theory Teaches Us About the Internet." *Communication and Critical Cultural Studies*, 11, no. 3 (2014): 274-275.

18. Chess & Shaw, "A Conspiracy of Fishes," 209-210.

19. Consalvo, "The monsters next door."

20. Leigh Alexander, "Milo Yiannopoulos: Twitter banning one man won't undo his poisonous legacy." *The Guardian* (2016, July 21). Retrieved from https://www.theguardian.com/technology/2016/jul/20/milo-yiannopoulos-twitter-ban-leslie-jones-bad-idea

21. Autobótika, *Afterlife Empire* (Steam, 2015).

22. @TFYCapitalists, "Final Total from the referal link is $23,601 from /v/ and 4chan" [Tweet] (2014, 12 September). Retrieved from: https://twitter.com/TFYCapitalists/status/510137763161968640

23. Dustin Kidd and Amanda J. Turner, "The #GamerGate files: Misogyny in the media." In Alison Novak and Imaani Jamillah El-Burki (Eds.). *Defining identity and the changing scope of culture in the digital age* (Hershey: IGI Global, 2016): 124-126.

24. /v/ Vivian James Archive [reddit forum] (2014). Retrieved from: http://i.imgur.com/9HPJZh8.jpg

25./v/ Vivian James Archive

26. Escapist Magazine Forum (2014), accessed from: http://www.escapistmagazine.com/forums/jump/6.860805.21409096

27. Escapist Magazine Forum.

28. Escapist Magazine Forum.

29. Golding and Van Deventer, *Game changers*, 184.

30. Salter and Blodgett, "Hypermasculinity & Dickwolves."

31. Salter and Blodgett, "Hypermasculinity & Dickwolves," 409.

32. /v/ Vivian James Archive

33. Salter and Blodgett, "Hypermasculinity & Dickwolves.

34. Matt Lees, "What Gamergate should have taught us about the 'Alt-right.'" *The Guardian* (2016, 1 December). Retrieved from https://www.theguardian.com/technology/2016/dec/01/gamergate-alt-right-hate-trump

35. Gray et al. "Blurring the boundaries," 3.

36. Judith Butler, *Gender Trouble* (New York: Routledge, 1990), 178.

"SHUT UP AND PLAY" FIGURES

Figure 1: Original crowdsourced custom character design of Vivian James created on /v/ for the The Fine Young Capitalists and the game *Afterlife Empire* (Autobótika, 2015), accessed from: http://i0.kym-cdn.com/entries/icons/original/000/016/296/image.jpg

Figure 2: Vivian James and her unofficial tagline: "shut up and play", accessed from: http://i0.kym-cdn.com/photos/images/original/000/838/944/f70.gif

DIGITAL CAPTURE NOTES

1. Gruber, Otto von. "Photogrammetry." *Collected lectures and essays* (translated from German by GT McCaw and FA Cazelet), Am. Photographic Publ. Co., Boston (1932).

2. Since SfM can progressively refine models as more images are added, it allows for a method of understanding and reconstructing an environment known as Simultaneous Locating and Mapping (SLAM). In applications of SLAM, a robot, for example, can build up a 3D map of a previously unknown environment as it moves through it, both learning about the space, and locating its position within it at the same time. *See* Azarbayejani, Ali, and Alex P. Pentland. "Recursive estimation of motion, structure, and focal length." *IEEE Transactions on Pattern Analysis & Machine Intelligence* 6 (1995): 562-575.

3. B. Curless, N. Snavely, M. Goesele, S. M. Seitz and H. Hoppe, "Multi-View Stereo for Community Photo Collections," *2007 11th IEEE International Conference on Computer Vision (ICCV)*, Rio de Janeiro, 2007, pp. 1-8.

4. Once outlier regions of the photogrammetry reconstruction had been removed. Toschi, I., P. Rodríguez-Gonzálvez, F. Remondino, S. Minto, S. Orlandini, and A. Fuller. "Accuracy evaluation of a mobile mapping system with advanced statistical methods." *The International Archives of Photogrammetry, Remote Sensing and Spatial Information Sciences 40*, no. 5 (2015): 245

5. Emphasis in original. von Brevern, Jan. "Fototopografía: The "Futures Past" of Surveying." *Intermédialités: Histoire et théorie des arts, des lettres et des techniques/Intermediality: History and Theory of the Arts, Literature and Technologies 17* (2011): 53-67.

6. Willis, Mark. "How to create a Digital Elevation Model from Photosynth point clouds." *Blog: Markaeology* (2010). http://palentier.blogspot.com/2010/12/how-to-create-digital-elevationmodel.html. Last accessed 15 September 2018

7. Davis, Annabelle, David Belton, Petra Helmholz, Paul Bourke, and Jo McDonald. "Pilbara rock art: laser scanning, photogrammetry and 3D photographic reconstruction as heritage management tools." *Heritage Science 5*, no. 1 (2017): 25.

8. Latour, Bruno. *Science in action: How to follow scientists and engineers through society.* Harvard university press, 1987.

9. Harle, Joshua.(2013) "Emerging Topologies: Tours and Maps of Augmented Space." *PhD diss.*, Faculty of Fine Arts, University of New South Wales.

10. *Ibid.*, 56.

11. Tomas, David. *Beyond the image machine: a history of visual technologies.* A&C Black, 2004, 162.

12. Latour, Bruno. *Science in action: How to follow scientists and engineers through society.* Harvard university press, 1987, 10.

13. *Ibid.*, 12-23.

14. Løvlie, Anders Sundnes. "The rhetoric of persuasive games: freedom and discipline in America's Army." *Master's thesis*, 2007.

15. e.g. "I see" for understanding, "illuminating or enlightening" for informative, "transparent" or "opaque" for easy or difficult to get knowledge of.

16. Pallasmaa, Juhani. (2008). *The Eyes of the Skin : Architecture and the Senses.* Hoboken, NJ, John Wiley & Sons, 19.

17. El Antably, Ahmed. "The Virtual (Re) Construction of History: Some Epistemological Questions." UC Berkeley: *The Proceedings of Spaces of History / Histories of Space: Emerging Approaches to the Study of the Built Environment*, (2010). Retrieved from https://escholarship.org/uc/item/225426rr

18. von Brevern, Jan. "Fototopografia: The "Futures Past" of Surveying." *Intermédialités: Histoire et théorie des arts, des lettres et des techniques/Intermediality: History and Theory of the Arts, Literature and Technologies* 17 (2011): 53-67.

19. Turnbull, David. *Masons, tricksters and cartographers: Comparative studies in the sociology of scientific and indigenous knowledge.* Taylor & Francis, 2003, 11

20. Shields, Rob. *The virtual.* Routledge, 2005, 61.

21. Harle, Josh. "Emerging Topologies." *PhD diss.*, Faculty of Fine Arts, University of New South Wales (2013), 93.

22. Latour, Bruno and Albena Yaneva. "Give Me a Gun and I Will Make All Buildings Move: An Ant's View of Architecture," *Explorations in architecture: Teaching, design, research* (2008): 84.

23. Bousquet, Antoine, "The Perspectival Eye", *Glass Bead Journal*, (2018) retrieved from http://www.glass-bead.org/research-platform/the-perspectival-eye/

24. Manovich, Lev, et al. (2001). *The Language of New Media*, MIT Press, 200.

25. *Ibid.*, 201.

26. von Brevern, Jan. "Fototopografia: The "Futures Past" of Surveying." *Intermédialités: Histoire et théorie des arts, des lettres et des techniques/Intermediality: History and Theory of the Arts, Literature and Technologies* 17 (2011): 53-67.

27. Kelly, Andy, "What virtual toilets can teach us about the art of game design", *PCGamer*, (2016), retrieved from https://www.pcgamer.com/what-virtual-toilets-can-teach-us-about-the-art-of-game-design/

28. Latour, Bruno. *Science in action: How to follow scientists and engineers through society.* Harvard university press, 1987, 100.

29. de Certeau, Michel. (2002). *The Practice of Everyday Life.* Los Angeles, University of California Press, 200.

30. Harle, Josh. "Decolonising the Map", *Openism Journal* (2016).

31. My emphasis, de Certeau, M. (2002). *The Practice of Everyday Life.* Los Angeles, University of California Press, 35.

32. Snavely, Noah, Steven M. Seitz, and Richard Szeliski. "Photo tourism: exploring photo collections in 3D." In *ACM transactions on graphics (TOG)*, vol. 25, no. 3, pp. 835-846. ACM, 2006.

33. Gruber, Otto von. "Photogrammetry." *Collected lectures and essays* (translated from German by GT McCaw and FA Cazelet), Am. Photographic Publ. Co., Boston (1932).

34. Mogel, Lize, and Alexis Bhagat, eds. *An atlas of radical cartography.* Journal of Aesthetics & Protest Press, 2008.

DIGITAL CAPTURE FIGURES

Figure 1: Dense surface model of Lord Botetourt statue at the College of William and Mary. Photogrammetry experiment processed in Agisoft "Photoscan", Attribution: Edward Triplett

Figure 2: A coloured reconstruction of a street in Paris produced using the photogrammetry software *Capturing Reality*, Attribution: Josh Harle

Figure 3: The same model without colour or cleanup, showing areas of limited reconstruction data as 'blobs', Attribution: Josh Harle

Figure 4: PhotoSynth 'photo tourism' navigator example, Attribution: Josh Harle & Murujuga Aboriginal Corporation

Figure 5: Screenshot from *Palimpsest – Collective memory through Virtual Reality*, illustrating digital capture used in creative projects, Created by J Russell Beaumont, Haavard Tveito, and Takashi Torisu with the Interactive Architecture Lab at the Bartlett School of Architecture, University College London. Attribution: J Russell Beaumont, Haavard Tveito, and Takashi Torisu

BEYOND IMPERIAL TOOLS NOTES

1. Otherwise known as The Dreaming, and or, Jukupurra, and akin to Law.

2. Lewis, *Making Kin With The Machines.*

3. Jackson 2Bears, *A Conversation With Spirits Inside The Simulation Of A Coast Salish Longhouse.*

4. Technologies which solve problems through meaningful scientific or technological innovation.

5. Graham, Some *Thoughts About The Philosophical Underpinnings Of Aboriginal Worldviews.*

6. Ibid.

7. Abdilla & Fitch, *Indigenous Knowledge Systems And Pattern Thinking: An Expanded Analysis -Of The First Indigenous Robotics Prototype Workshop.*

8. Otherwise known within A.I as related to the field of machine learning where patterns and regularities within data are recognised through unsupervised learning.

9. From the *Wiradjuri* language

10. Mukgrrngal / Wayne Armytage, Elder and Lore man.

11. Abdilla & Fitch, *Indigenous Knowledge Systems And Pattern Thinking: An Expanded Analysis Of The First Indigenous Robotics Prototype Workshop.*

12. Alison Page, in conversation 2018.

13. Kidman, *The Australian Da Vinci: How David Unaipon (Almost) Changed Our Nation.*

14. Lardil Elders Kelly Bunbujee and Jackson Jacob speaking in Memmott, Paul. "Rainbows, story places, and malkri sickness in the North Wellesley Islands." *Oceania* 53, no. 2 (1982): 163-182.

15. Pronounced noon-oo

16. Office of Environment and Heritage.

17. Ibid.

18. I.e. meeting of localised languages and governance systems, known as Nations.

19. *Office of Environment and Heritage.*

20. White, *Native Spinifex Set To Bring Big Returns To Australia's Outback - Via Better Condoms.*

21. *Global 3D Printing Market Size 2018/2021 - via Statistic.*

22. Memmott, *Nanotechnology and the Dreamtime Knowledge of Spinifex Grass.*

23. Vandana, *Biotechnological Development And The Conservation Of Biodiversity.*

24. In conversation propositions for Pattern Thinking adaptations: Crighton Nichols, Steven J. Taylor and Josh Harle.

25. Chaturvedi, *LinkedIn*.

26. Deep Neural Networks.

27. Don Hill, *Listening To Stones: Learning In Leroy Little Bear's Laboratory: Dialogue In The World Outside*

28. Old Ways, New.

29. Ito, *Resisting Reduction: A Manifesto*.

Graham, *Some Thoughts About The Philosophical Underpinnings Of Aboriginal Worldviews*

BEYOND IMPERIAL TOOLS FIGURES

Figure 1: Boomerang (Musée d'ethnographie de Genève), Attribution: Rama (Wikimedia Commons User) / CC-BY-SA

Figure 2: Photograph by unattributed studio. Tyrell Collection, Powerhouse Museum, Sydney. 85/1286-721,00g0003

Figure 3: Tussock at State Highway 94 between Mossburn and The Key NZ, Attribution: Ulrich Lange

BEYOND IMPERIAL TOOLS BIBLIOGRAPHY

2014. "Brewarrina Aboriginal Fish Traps / Baiame's Nguunhu". *Office of Environment and Heritage*. http://www.environment.nsw.gov.au/heritageapp/ViewHeritageItemDetails.aspx?ID=5051305

2Bears, Jackson. 2018. "A Conversation With Spirits Inside The Simulation Of A Coast Salish Longhouse | Ctheory". *Ctheory.Net*. http://ctheory.net/ctheory_wp/a-conversation-with-spirits-inside-the-simulation-of-a-coast-salish-longhouse/.

Chaturvedi, Swati. 2015. *Linkedin*. https://www.linkedin.com/pulse/so-what-exactly-deep-technology-swati-chaturvedi/.

Abdilla, Angie, and Robert Fitch (aff 1). 2017. "FCJ-209 Indigenous Knowledge Systems And Pattern Thinking: An Expanded Analysis Of The First Indigenous Robotics Prototype Workshop". *Twentyeight.Fibreculturejournal.org*.

"Global 3D Printing Market Size 2018/2021 | Statistic". 2018. *Statista*. https://www.statista.com/statistics/590113/worldwide-market-for-3d-printing/.

Graham, Mary. 1999. "Some Thoughts About The Philosophical Underpinnings Of Aboriginal Worldviews". *Worldviews: Global Religions, Culture, And Ecology* 3 (2): 105-118.

Hill, Don. 2008. "Listening To Stones: Learning In Leroy Little Bear's Laboratory: Dialogue In The World Outside". *The Magazine For Engaged Citizens*.

Ito, Joichi. 2018. "Resisting Reduction: A Manifesto". *MIT* Press, Resisting Reduction: A Manifesto https://jods.mitpress.mit.edu/pub/resisting-reduction.

Kidman, Angus. 2018. "The Australian Da Vinci: How David Unaipon (Almost) Changed Our Nation". *Gizmodo*. https://www.gizmodo.com.au/2014/03/the-australian-da-vinci-how-david-unaipon-almost-changed-our-nation/

Lewis, Jason. 2018. "Making Kin With The Machines – Jason Edward Lewis – Medium". *Medium*. https://medium.com/@jaspernotwell/making-kin-with-the-machines-a5aaebe4e3f2.

Memmott, P., D. Martin, and N. Amiralian. "Nanotechnology and the Dreamtime Knowledge of Spinifex Grass." *Green Composites*, 2017, 181-98.

Memmott, Paul. "Rainbows, Story Places, and Malkri Sickness in the North Wellesley Islands." *Oceania*53, no. 2 (1982): 163-82.

Shiva, Vandana. 2018. "Biotechnological Development And The Conservation Of Biodiversity". *Biopolitics: A Feminist And Ecological Reader On Biopolitics*, 193-199. Accessed June 1.

White, Merran. 2018. "Native Spinifex Set To Bring Big Returns To Australia's Outback - Via Better Condoms". *Ag Innovators*. http://www.aginnovators.org.au/news/native-spinifex-set-bring-big-returns-australias-outback-better-condoms.

COLLISIONS IMAGE CREDITS

In order of appearance:

1. Photo Credit: Piers Mussared

2. *Behind-the-scenes of the Collisions production.* Photo Credit: Piers Mussared

3. *Nyarri tries virtual reality for the first time.* Photo Credit: Pete Brundle

4. Photo Credit: Piers Mussared

5. *"Spirit Cloud"* Artwork by Jossie Malis, spirit cloud imagery Lynette Wallworth.

6. *Liam recording fire sounds.* Photo Credit: Piers Mussared

7. *Collisions.* Photo Credit: Piers Mussared

8. *The Jaunt virtual reality camera on a drone over a landscape of fires burning spinifex, an ancient Martu land management practice.* Photo Credit: Piers Mussared

PROJECT BIRRONGGAI IMAGE CREDITS

In order of appearance:

1. *Render of the Biame.* Image Credit: Jeremy Worrall / Frenetic Studios

2. *Wugan the Dream guide.* Image Credit: Jeremy Worrall / Frenetic Studios

3. *The Alter at which Wugan draws in the pathways through the Dreamtime allowing you to travel between realms (level selector).* Image Credit: Jeremy Worrall / Frenetic Studios

4. *Wugan accessing the Rites stone (level select).* Image Credit: Jeremy Worrall / Frenetic Studios

5. *Turntable shot of Wugan; An extension of Biame Wugan follows you through the Dreamtime guiding you on your journey and bridging the gap between realms.* Image Credit: Jeremy Worrall / Frenetic Studios

6. *Render of the playzone in its infancy, features Biame and the home tree.* Image Credit: Jeremy Worrall / Frenetic Studios

7. *Another perspective shot.* Image Credit: Jeremy Worrall / Frenetic Studios

8. *Original Concept for the play zone, a chunk of earth lifted into the heavens by Biame the ancient all father and sky god. This is the centre piece for the players adventure.* Image Credit: Jeremy Worrall / Frenetic Studios

BARANGAROO NGANGAMAY IMAGE CREDITS

In order of appearance:

1. *Barangaroo Ngangamay Augemented Reality activated postcards*, Photo Credit: Bonnie Elliott

2. *Sharon Mason throwing a fishing line.* Image Credit: Bonnie Elliott

3. *Barangaroo Ngangamay App Point of Interest marker.* Image Credit: Bonnie Elliott/ A-Positive

4. *Using the app onsite at Barangaroo Reserve.* Photo Credit: A-Positive

5. *Barrugin - echidna rock engraving at Barangaroo Reserve..* Photo Credit: Bonnie Elliott

THALU IMAGE CREDITS

In order of appearance:

1. *Thalu project poster.* Image Credit: FrameVR / Tyson Mowarin

2. *The fauna Thalu* (screenshot). Image Credit: FrameVR / Tyson Mowarin

3. *Moving between Thalu sites* (screenshot). Image Credit: FrameVR / Tyson Mowarin

4. *Gathering at the fish Thalu* (screenshot). Image Credit: FrameVR / Tyson Mowarin

5. *The entrance to the fish Thalu, Pilbara* (screenshot). Image Credit: FrameVR / Tyson Mowarin

TORRES STRAIT VIRTUAL REALITY IMAGE CREDITS

In order of appearance:

1. *Baidam the Shark Constellation* (screenshot). Image credit: Rhett Loban

2. *Wawa the Giant* (screenshot). Image credit: Rhett Loban

3. *Tombstone* (screenshot). Image credit: Rhett Loban

4. *Kupas the Dogai Slayer* (screenshot). Image credit: Rhett Loban

5. *Sunrise on Mabuiag Island* (screenshot). Image credit: Rhett Loban

6. *Kai Reef During the Day* (screenshot). Image credit: Rhett Loban

7. *Kai Reef at Night* (screenshot). Image credit: Rhett Loban

8. *Rhett playing Torres Strait Virtual Reality* (screenshot). Photo credit: Rhett Loban

www.ingramcontent.com/pod-product-compliance
Lightning Source LLC
Chambersburg PA
CBHW040903180526
45159CB00010BA/2909